Swedish Cooking

Swedish Cooking

ICA BOKFÖRLAG

ICA bokförlag
721 85 Västerås
www.forlaget.ica.se/bok

ICA Förlaget är miljöcertifierat enligt ISO 14001

© 1995 ICA Förlaget AB Västerås
14th edition
First edition published 1971, seventh printing 2004

Text about history and food traditions: Marianne Sandberg

Recipes: ICA Provkök (ICA Test Kitchen)

Translation: Pamela Danielson-Theurer

Photography: Kent Jardhammar, Bildproduktion, Hans B Eriksson, Bildproduktion, Stig Holm

Illustrations: Olaus Magnus *Historia de gentibus septentrionalis* 1555

Cover design: Paul Eklund

Printed in Italy by Graphicom 2004

ISBN 91-534-1595-7

Contents

Preface

"Swedish Cooking" contains almost 150 recipes for typically Swedish dishes, including main courses, breads, cakes, and desserts. Most of them are everyday favorites or foods traditionally associated with different holidays such as Easter, Midsummer, or Christmas.

Today Swedish food has become more international, featuring both Italian pasta as well as oriental dishes using a wok. Such recipes haven't been included in this volume however. No, the main thrust of this book is devoted to what we usually call husmanskost (old-fashioned Swedish homecooking) and is composed of very traditional and commonplace dishes. However, an occasional newfangled recipe using Swedish ingredients has found its way into this collection.

At the end of the book you will find a glossary that lists and explains many of the dishes found herein. It also includes some of the ordinary grocery items found in Sweden.

Conversions

Both American and metric measurements are given in the recipes found in this book. All measurements are approximate and have been converted from metric to American. Moreover, the recipes have been tested using Swedish groceries. If you use grocery items from another country to prepare recipes from this book, the proportions of the ingredients might need some adjustment. In order to help simplify the process of conversion, a table of Swedish weights per 100 ml for Swedish food staples has been included.

1 qt = 4 cups = 950 ml
1 cup = 8 fl oz = 237 ml
1 fl oz = 29,6 ml
100 ml = 0,42 cup
1 liter = 1000 ml = 1,05 qt

1 pound = 454 g
1 ounce = 28 g
100 g = 0,2 lb

Swedish groceries, weights per 100 ml

All-purpose flour 60 g
Brown sugar 70 g
Cocoa 40 g
Coffee 40 g
Icing sugar 60 g
Nuts, shelled 65 g
Oat meal 35 g
Oil 90 g
Potato flour 80 g
Raisins 60 g
Rice 85 g
Rye flour 55 g
Salt 125 g
Sugar 85 g
Syrup 140 g
Wholemeal flour 60 g

Oven Temperatures

°Celsius	°Fahrenheit
100–150	212–300
175–225	350–425
250	475
275	525

°C into °F: multiply by 9, divide by 5, add 32
°F into °C: subtract 32, multiply by 5, divide by 9

A History of Swedish Cuisine

When a Swede hears the word *husmanskost* (old-fashioned homecooking), his mind immediately conjures up an image of a kitchen where the art of cooking stands supreme. One senses the aroma of hearty stews and envisages simmering saucepans. Crispy brown Baltic herring dance about lightly in a heated skillet. Splendid roasts and game tantalize us from the oven, provided it isn't already filled with huge loaves of leavened bread or moist spongecake. Here one can always find a tasty morsel on which to nibble. Yes, here is a great source of warmth and security.

At any rate, we like to believe that this was the way it once was. However, in days gone by food was by no means as greatly varied as the fare of today.

Nowadays we are able to prepare both common foods, as well as those for special occasions, in a manner that neither our grandparents nor even our mothers could possibly dream.

Sweden is fortunate to have a long coastline and many lakes, thereby ensuring its inhabitants of a great diversity of fish ranging from Baltic herring to cod and salmon.

Meat, on the other hand, was a scarce commodity in kitchens of the past. While hunting did make an additional contribution in sections of the country covered by forest, more of an emphasis was put on raising dairy cattle than on meat production. There also existed big game such as moose, as well as quite a bit of poultry and small game such as hare and rabbit.

Husmanskost was simple and concerned itself mostly with porridge and gruel, combs and black pudding, cabbage soup, and dried fish. Every home put aside its own larder from what was harvested from the garden. There wasn't a great deal of cash in circulation in those days nor an abundance of stores from which to shop everyday.

It wasn't until the middle of the 1800's that Swedes were allowed to open country stores. These stores sold salt herring, a few spices, treacle, coffee, and maybe even a little loaf sugar. However merchandise was purchased mostly by bartering instead of paying with cash.

On the other hand, city dwellers could go shopping at the grocers, the butchers, or the bakers. Moreover, they had large pantries and food cellars in which they could stock up to a years supply of certain staples. Yet, city residents could still remain farmers — by farming on town land!

Salted and dried food constituted the basis of Swedish homecooking. Even today we, Swedes, prefer a lightly smoked ham at Christmas rather than a fresh one. We also think that the pork knuckles which complement our pea soup or mashed turnips should be pickled. Otherwise the food won't taste right! Taking into consideration all that salted food,

Bundles of dried fish and barrels filled with salted and dried fish.

it's no wonder so much beer and ale were consumed long ago!

Prior to the arrival of the canning apparatus and freezers, dehydration and fermentation were two typical methods of food preservation .

Ölsupa was a very common dish previously; it consisted of a soup made from stale bread that had been thoroughly soaked in beer or a derivative thereof. *Supamaten,* which means all types of soups, was a good way of using leftovers and making food last.

In 1755 Cajsa Warg's book, "A Guide to Housekeeping for Young Women", was published, and there we are already able to trace the influence of French cuisine in that which we today consider typically Swedish. Many new cookbooks were published during the nineteenth century and contributed to variation in Swedish homecooking.

Cajsa Warg gave a great deal of advice on the care of stored food.

First she lists everything that is pickled: meat, pork, salmon, salt herring, Baltic herring, small codfish, pike, and eel. Then she continues with all the dried fish: stockfish, flounder, whiting, and pike. Everything that hasn't been consumed during winter must be brought out and brushed clean from moths.

Yellow and green peas (which couldn't be purchased pre-dried yet), hard bread, flatbread, and even meat were also dried. Salted and dried mutton and reindeer meat gave stews and bouillon an especially tasty flavor.

The first one heard of *surströmming* (fermented Baltic herring) was in a tax-roll from the 1500's where it was written that every fifteenth barrel was to fall to the crown. Some are even of the opinion that the Thirty Year War was won thanks to a little help from *surströmming.* When it arrived at the battlefront the soldiers were besides themselves with joy and ate as if there was no tommorow. Then they went into battle and breathed on the enemy.......

I can't vouch for whether or not this was actually true; however, it is a fact that there was a shortage of salt in Sweden at that time. On the coast of Northern

Spearfishing salmon in a river during the Middle Ages. The salmon was the smoked over an open fire.

Sweden, those who worked with preserving Baltic herring discovered a method to preserve the fish yet only used an absolute minimum of salt in the process.

This method still exists today - although the fermentation process is carried out under strict control indoors and not outside in fresh air as before.

Baltic herring is caught from May to the beginning of June. This is its spawning season, and the herring is of high quality. Then the herring is fermented and, according to a royal ordinance, first ready to be eaten the third week of August.

Milk was also a sensitive perishable. In fact, it was only during the summer, after spring calving, that milk was plentiful. Just before midsummer cattle, calves, and sheep were driven up to mountain pastures by shepardesses and didn't return again to the farms until autumn. The young women passed away the time up in the mountains by making cheese, cooking whey-cheese, as well as processing a type of thick sour milk.

Carl von Linné described how he ran across a form of "stringy milk" in the province of Ångermansland in his narrative, "A Trip to Lappland in 1732". According to Linné, this was made from the whey after the process of curdling had been completed. The milk was so glue-like that "one could pull it like a string from wall to wall." In Västerbotten he was even served salted and sun-dried breast of woodgrouse. Moreover, he observed, "crayfish and fleas didn't exist in Lappland."

Out in the country, porridge and gruel were the dominate food in the average Swedish household, albeit a fine manor house or an ordinary farmhouse. Most often porridge was made fresh in the evening and eaten for supper. In the morning the leftovers were fried and served with syrup, something the children loved. Porridge was served everyday as well as on special occasions. One carefully separated the two types: Simple porridge was prepared with water and served with lingonberries; "white porridge" was a more festive, milk-based, porridge. The custom of dining on rice pudding on Christmas Eve is a carry-over from days gone by.

Swedes still follow the tradition of taking porridge, *flyttgröt*, with them when they first visit someone who has just moved to a new address. Previously, new mothers were given post-delivery porridge after the birth of a baby.

Barley porridge was common in Norrland and Northern Svealand, while rye porridge dominated elsewhere. During this period, proper porridge was thick and filling. Watery porridge was classified as "gentlemen's porridge." However, one could never be sure of having milk with porridge. Water mixed with honey, syrup, whey, or even beverages mixed with milk or water were some of the different liquids used in the making of porridge. Sometimes meat or fish bouillon and even lingon in water could be served with porridge.

We are used to eating porridge from our own bowl. However, far into the 1940's one could find porridge being eaten from a common bowl in different areas of Sweden, among other places in Southern Lappland. On the other hand everyone always had his own bowl for the liquid (*grötväta*) that was to complement the porridge. If the porridge was especially fine, a dab of butter was dropped in a hole made in the middle.

Chips of dried whey butter or cheese soaked in water were either served as gruel or blended into a white sauce to lend extra flavor to common food. Our Northern provinces still practice this custom today when they season the gravy of game roasts with a little piece of whey cheese.

Unleavened bread is also an early discovery. The dough, which might have originated as a clump of porridge, was first flattened out on a stone and then heated until the water evaporated from it. This type of bread exists all over the world and has the advantage that it keeps a long time. In Sweden one used to say, "what's baked for the christening will keep till the wedding."

Nonetheless, one also celebrated with "birthing beer, "bridal beer", "burial beer", etc. so that scholars still debate which came first: the bread or the beer? Could it possibly be that thirst was a greater drive than hunger? Probably the earliest grains were more suitable for brewing beer than baking bread, and in most countries one brewed beer that was both nutritious, thirst quenching, and yet low in calories.

The Swedes can, in fact, thank some of their kings for many of the dishes which they consider to be typically Swedish. For example, without Gustav Wasa and his "import" of skillful miners, we wouldn't have *falukorv* today. A great many oxen were needed in order to pull up the baskets from the Falu copper mines. When they no longer had the strength to work as draught animals, they were slaughtered. Their hide was used for making belts for the miners as well as for the baskets which transported the copper ore up from within the mines. The meat of the oxen was used for roasts and other delicacies for the hungry miners. However, even the smaller pieces of meat and intestines didn't go to waste. Among others, miners coming from Belgium and Germany, made their native sausage. It was quickly christened *falukorv*, and became so popular that it was later sold at marketplaces. In Germany we can find one of the forefathers of *falukorv* in the sausage called Thüringer Bratwurst.

If we can believe a royal letter to a bailiff named Jöran Jönsson, in 1562, Gustav Vasa's son, King Erik XIV, was the first crayfish lover in Sweden. The King wanted "a huge heap of crayfish" for both his guests at the castle as well as for a wedding.

The descending Vasa kings also liked crayfish very much. This is probably due to the fact that by then Italian cuisine even influenced the kitchen of the royal family. One had eaten crayfish on the continent for a long time, and the monastaries (even those in Sweden) had their own crayfish catchers. Crayfish were used for both food and medicine.

However, it wasn't until the 1700's that crayfish and the notion of crayfish parties spread to the country estates throughout Sweden and were eulogized by Bellman in many of his ballads. Moreover, it wasn't until the twentieth century that crayfish parties became widespread throughout all of Sweden, starting first in Svealand and Northern Götaland. It was also then that all the paraphernalia such as paper moons, special plates and cutlery, especially woven crayfish-striped tablecloths, and handblown glass decanters in the form of dogs or pigs etc. appeared.

There is another favorite dish that is of royal origin. King Carl XII and his soldiers were imprisoned in Bender, Turkey, for many years. There, the King and his men tasted *dolmar* which were made from mutton wrapped in grape leaves. In Turkish *dolmar* means cloak and refers to the wrapping of the grape leave. When the warriors eventually returned to Sweden, they took with them the recipe for *dolmar*. However, now the commonplace cabbage leaf was substituted for the grape leaf. The rice used in this recipe still reminds us of the oriental heritage of this dish. According to research carried out by the royal restaurateur Tore Wretman, the custom of dining on *"kåldomar"* began in Stockholm. A group of Turkish officials traveled to Stockholm to press the King for money – and then stayed on for several years!

Cajsa Warg's recipe for *"kåldomar"* contains a mixture of minced veal and rice seasoned with pepper, nutmeg, salt, onion, and a little cloves. She writes that this mixure is then wrapped in grape leaves, but if none are available "one can use cabbage leaves instead."

Sweet desserts weren't very prevalent in the everyday diet, but during berry season one gorged on "berry pudding" which actually was something of a cross between a pudding and a thickened soup. In Småland, Hälsingland, Västerbotten, and Norbotten thin rounds of rye or even sometimes wheat were baked and then filled with a thick layer of blueberries or lingonberries. However, in those days the most common dessert, and evening meal as well sometimes, was lingonberries and milk.

The potato had already made its way to Sweden by the 1600's, and the first recipes turned up in 1664. However, Jonas Alströmer is considered to be the father of the Swedish potato. In 1733 he wrote that one could boil, mash, and even mix the potato with flour, a technique used for making potato dumplings.

The potato didn't really gain popularity, however, until the Duchess Eva de la Gardie discovered the art of distilling aquavit from potatoes, thereby saving the invaluable grain for food. In 1748 Eva de la Gardie was the first woman to be elected into the Swedish Academy of Science. In her writings she pointed out that one could also make flour and even powder from potatoes.

Despite the fact that farmers first thought the potato to be tasteless in comparison to the turnip and carrot, it didn't take long before the potato definitely became the number one staple in Sweden. In many homes throughout the country the only dinner food available was herring fins, potatoes, and lingonberries. Many different varieties of potatoes became available: rosy red, yellow, white, and blue..... and they could be mealy, juicy, dry, or sometimes even a little leathery. Certain types reminded us of the present day "almond potato," a favorite of the inhabitants of Northern Sweden. In Västergötland, near Falköping, one developed a local sort that was scaly like asparagus. Today, the indigo blue Congo potato has become popular, especially with professional chefs.

Potatoes are a major industry today. Just think about those early spring potatoes grown on the Bjäre

Baking crisp bread over an open fire on an iron griddle during the 1500's.

peninsula in Skåne. Swedes delight in eating these steaming, new-boiled potatoes together with just a dab of butter and a little salt!

During the rest of the year potatoes are served as a complement to other foods, but can even turn up in the form of old favorites such as potato pancakes or potato dumplings. Modern industry has converted the potato into many different forms ranging from potato chips to potato au gratin that can be heated either in a regular oven or a microwave.

Perhaps, we haven't given much thought to the fact that one of the most revolutionary inventions of industrialization was the cast-iron stove, the forerunner of our modern day range. By the mid-1800's it had become widespread and made food preparation much easier compared to preparing food in a big kettle over an open hearth. Cast-iron stoves were a very comfortable source of heat in the kitchen and also encouraged home baking in an entirely new way.

Previously, one baked in large open ovens located in bakeries that were separate from the main house, something which is still customary today in our Northern provinces. One baked only a few times a year, usually at Christmas and in late spring. On those occasions, which lasted for several days each, one baked a household's entire bread supply for the coming months. Often all the women in the village baked together.

With the onset of cast-iron stoves one could bake more often and make smaller portions of bread, buns, and cakes. Coffee klatches became a way of socializing and still exist today. Nowadays, a guest isn't offered such a broad selection of rusk, sweet yeast breads, cakes, and several different types of cookies as frequently as was the fashion 30 or 40 years ago.

You might wonder about the smorgasbord. Surely it must be included within the realm of Swedish homecooking. Yes, for celebrations and mostly at restaurants. Our Christmas smorgasbord and those found on other major holidays are a simplified form that still exists today.

The origin of the Swedish *smörgåsbord* can be traced back to the so-called *brännvinsbordet*, a little cocktail (schnapps) buffet which started off dinner in days gone by. The men usually gathered in the corner of the dining or living room. They enjoyed a schnapps with a little salt on the side. Now and then the ladies might be offered a sugar cube soaked in aquavit.

If one visits the Nordiska Museet in Stockholm one can see a reconstructed *brännvinsbord*, beautifully set with a stiffly ironed damask tablecloth, a chest filled with small bottles for different sorts of aquavit, some of them personally flavored perhaps. Popular schnapps flavorings were wormwood, sweet gale, caraway, southern wood, as well as bitter orange. Moreover, the table should be set with pickled anchovies from young herring, a well-ripened cheese, and salted pretzels on which to munch.

Swedish restaurants have experienced a renaissance of the smorgasbord, especially during the tourist season! Therefore, it is extremely important that competent personnel is available to help instruct tourists on the etiquette of enjoying a smorgasbord. For the sake of orientation, one should take a stroll around the entire buffet first in order to see the many different types of delicacies available. Then one should return to the smorgasbord at least four or five times in order to avoid mixing the different types of food and tastes too much.

Foods and Festivals in Sweden

Christmas

A Swedish Christmas is a cross between both heathen and Christian traditions. The actual word for Christmas, *jul*, can be traced back to Old Swedish. During heathen times we celebrated a midwinter sacrifice at about the time of the winter solstice, the day when the sun returned to the northern latitudes.

It wasn't difficult for the wise and ingenious priests to puzzle together both the heathen and Christian beliefs when Sweden became christianized. By approximately 100 A.D. the Church had already established December 25th to be the date of Jesus birth.

One can also explain why just Christmas ham wound up on the Christmas smorgasbord. The wild boar was probably tamed sometime during the Bronze Ages. Its meat was tender and succulent and soon became the cult animal of the Vikings. Valhalla was the Vikings paradise and where warriors met to hold nightly feasts. Every night they dined on a special boar named Sarimer which was roasted over an open pit. Beautiful amazons served *mjöd*, a beer brewed from honey and hops, to the warriors. Then, abracadabra, each morning lively little Sarimar reappeared in his pen once again, grunting happily and eagerly awaiting a new slaughter for the evening feast.

Dried fish, preferably cod and ling, were the Vikings most important provision during their long journies at sea. This eventually evolved into *lutfisk* and wasn't served more often during times of fasting than it is today. During the Catholic period in Sweden the Christmas fast wasn't over until Christmas Day. That is why we still dine on *lutfisk* on Christmas Eve.

Rice pudding is a later tradition. People used to put both coins and small figurines of the Christ Child in the pudding; nowadays we sometimes use an almond instead. The one who gets the almond – and has come of age – will marry during the coming year. In addition, everyone must try to make up a little verse while eating the pudding. No poet laureate has ever emerged thanks to this tradition...but it's great fun!

The Swedish Christmas actually begins on December 13th with the celebration of Lucia, which combines a tradition from the Western part of Sweden together with an Italian saint. By the time *"lusse"* rolled around every year, all of the autumn farm chores of slaughtering, brewing, and baking had been completed. Both city dwellers and country residents had time to socialize now, and there was such an abundance of food that everyone - almost - was able to make a glutton of himself.

Our modern Christmas smorgasbord is very lavish but also features much fruit and greens, thereby making it much more balanced than its predecessor. We pickle two or three different kinds of herring and make homemade liver paté or sausage from family recipes handed down from one generation to the other. Now, however, we don't devour everything on a single occasion but rather spread out our dining enjoyment throughout the holiday season.

We have even begun to follow the Anglo-Saxon tradition of dining on turkey on Christmas Day, something unthinkable only 30 years ago. In every Swedish home there exists a special little pot filled with simmering spiced wine just waiting for guests who might pay a visit during the period from Lucia until *Tjugondag Knut*, that is to say January 13th, the day when Christmas is thrown out. This is literally the case now as this is the date when one usually throws out a Christmas tree that is shedding needles badly and seems to have done its part to enhance the Christmas season.

We exchange Christmas gifts on Christmas Eve. Our Swedish Santa is anglicized and allied to the Catholic Bishop Nicolaus, Santa Claus. In most Swedish families the father suddenly needs to run an errand at about four o'clock in the afternoon on Christmas Eve. While he's away, Santa usually shows up carrying his heavy sack......

Long ago the Christmas smorgasbords of different provinces distinguished themselves from one another. For example, in Hälsingland one churned much more butter at Christmas and moulded two cones in which a branched candle was placed. There was one branch for each family member. The butter from these cones was never eaten but remained on the table as a symbol of family fortune and was considered to be an extra blessing. In Hälsingland, one also ate a roast of veal seasoned with cloves instead of ham.

Easter

In Sweden, Easter has always been a Christian holiday; however the Pascal Lamb did cause a few problems for us. Easter usually precedes the lambing season in Sweden. Nevertheless lamb is often the main course on Easter Day. Luckily this is facilitated by Swedish meat regulations which stipulate that all sheep less than a year old are to be classified as lamb. This is also the time of year when chickens once again begin to lay. Eggs were "forbidden fruit" during Catholicism's Lent; therefore they were eaten with special indulgement on Easter. One gorged on eggs and egg dishes. In the Southern part of Sweden one played different types of games with eggs. Spring herring began to run, and salmon returned to spawn in Swedish rivers. Everything made its contribution to a splendid Easter smorgasbord. We paint Easter eggs by boiling them together with onion peel or special egg coloring and then decorate them according to our imagination – This is also part of the Swedish food tradition.

Good Friday was an extremely long and tedious day in Sweden previously, especially for the young. In 1969 the ban was lifted barring public entertainment on Good Friday. Now one can play music for easy listening, go to the movies or theater, or even arrange dances on what was previously such a solemn day. Nonetheless we still often serve fish (salmon) on Good Friday, a custom descending from our Catholic heritage.

Pentecost

Pentecost, like Easter, originates from Hebrew celebrations but became a Christian holiday during the first century and commemorates Christ's appearance before his disciples fifty days after his death. The Greek translation of the word pentecost is "the fiftieth day. Pentecost is called "the time of rapture" in the Nordic countries. That is not so peculiar since Pentecost always falls towards the end of spring when the days are filled with sunlight, and summer is just around the corner. Everything in nature is lush and green and in full bloom. One can go out and pick nettles for nettles soup, an old Swedish custom. Before, restaurants always had either spring chicken in cream sauce together with cucumber salad or dilled lamb with creamed morels on their spring menu. It goes without saying that dessert was, and still is, some variety of rhubarb, either a compote or a pie.

Midsummer

Perhaps Midsummer is the easiest of all Swedish holidays when it comes to food as the menu is practically given: matjes herring, spring potatoes with sour cream and chives. For dessert one enjoys fresh straw-

Crayfish and "Surströmming"

In the glow of bonfires, one celebrated Midsummer far into the night.

berries with whipped cream. In Skåne one likes to serve regular salt herring with chives in cream; however, matjes herring is often found as a sidedish.

In the beginning the Roman Catholic Church celebrated June 24th, Midsummer Day, in commemoration of the birthday of John the Baptist. After the Reformation the tradition continued, and Midsummer Day was celebrated on June 24th until 1953. After that Midsummer Day became a rotating holiday, with Midsummer Day falling on the first Saturday after the summer solstice. The custom of decorating a maypole and gathering to dance and play on Midsummer dates way back. Midsummer Eve was filled with mysticism. Young maidens picked 7 (or 9 depending on the custom) different sorts of flowers to put under their pillow in order to dream of their future husband that night. In some areas one collected special herbs and flowers during Midsummer, believing their medicinal powers would be enhanced. For the sake of good health, one gladly took a drink from a cold spring.

Around Midsummer, and in Northern Sweden especially, it was then that one put the cows out to pasture and seriously began to get under way with milking once again. It was then that one made the first processed sour cream of the season.

Foreign tourists visiting in August usually say that crayfish parties are the closest a Swede gets to really letting loose. Crayfish were once very common in our lakes and streams and were eaten year round. In the beginning of the 1900's a crayfish plague struck the original river crayfish. Therefore the plague-resistant signal crayfish was then introduced, and today we import crayfish from practically all over the world. The restriction forbidding frozen crayfish to be eaten prior to the second Thursday in August has been removed. Today the supply of Swedish crayfish is so minute that the former rules for a crayfish première have been abandoned. However, if one does trap fresh Swedish crayfish, the première regulations still apply, and the crayfish must be at least 10 cm in length from head to toe to be considered legal bounty.

The first crayfish parties were held by the middle-class during the latter part of the 1800's. In the beginning of the 1920's crayfish accessories such as funny hats, moon-shaped paper lanterns, special plates, tablecloths, and schnapps songs appeared.

The other major food festival in August is *surströmming* (fermented Baltic herring) which has its première the third Thursday of the month. *Surströmming* is served together with finely-diced onion (red and white), new boiled potatoes - preferably the yellow almond-shaped sort, and flatbread, both soft and hard. Beginners like to make *a klämma* (a type of sandwich roll) which is composed of a layer of sliced boiled potatoes, a layer of finely-diced onions, and finally a layer of fermented Baltic herring rolled-up in a piece of softly-buttered flatbread. Wash this down with beer. The aroma of fermented herring itself, is not worse than that of a well-ripened cheese, and many ardent *surströmming* lovers insist on being present when the can is opened and the odor leaks out!

Crayfish

Eel Feasts and St. Martin's Day

In Skåne one looks forward to the gloom of autumn with special anticipation. When the moon has waned in late August, it's time to get ready for eel parties. The first man and woman to catch a live eel from a dark barrel located in a darkened room are crowned king and queen of the party. The guests then feast on a myriad of different eel delicacies ranging from racked eel roasted over an open fire built from two different types of wood to straw-fried eel and eel in aspic.

One of the founders of the Swedish Academy of Gastronomy, author and lawyer Fritiof Nilsson (pseudonym "The Pirate") wrote many humorous stories about eel feasts. Today, as Swedes have become more mobile the customs of eel feasts as well as *surströmming* parties have become widespread throughout all of Sweden.

St. Martin's Day

This is another tradition from Southern Sweden that has worked its way northward. The geese in Skåne were nicely fattened and ready for slaughter just in time for St. Martin's Eve on November 10th. November 11th happens to be Martin Luther's names-day (Skåne is still the only Province in Sweden where the children are given the day off from school on November 10th!).

Legend says that in the town of Tours, France, there once was a pious and much-loved monk named Martin. He hid in a flock of geese to avoid being appointed bishop by the townspeople. The geese, of course, began to gaggle. The townspeople discovered Martin and, he eventually went on to become an excellent bishop. Every since then people slaughter and dine on goose on November 11th, all in his honor.

The dinner, itself, begins with black soup which is made from goose blood. Today people who don't care for black soup can opt for bouillon instead – although this is considered to be cheating just a bit! Stewed prunes, apples, red cabbage, and either boiled or baked potatoes complete the main course. Apple cake with a custard sauce is the classic dessert for this dinner. Then one is satiated!

Sandwiches

During the 1940's–1950's almost all elegant dinners commenced with an appetizer consisting of 3 different canapés or a small plate of cheese, herring, and butter, the latter being a remnant from the historical "brännvinsbordet". One served a modest cocktail patterned, for example, after the American Dry Martini, beer, and mineral water together with the small open-faced sandwiches. Beer or schnapps accompanied the plate of cheese and herring. The small canapés were later replaced by other types of appetizers. Today, however, the circle is complete, and once again many people enjoy serving canapés or cheese and herring as an appetizer.

Swedish sandwiches are always "open-faced." The Scandinavian airline, SAS, ran into a problem serving these sandwiches on their international flights in the beginning, as they were considered too fascinating by their competitors and thereby constituted unfair competition.

Liver Paté Sandwich
Smörgås med leverpastej

10 PORTIONS

1 tablespoon butter or margarine
2–3 slices of graham bread
10 small leaves of lettuce
¼ lb. (100 g) liver paté
¼ cup (50 g) coarsely grated pickled beets or gherkins
finely chopped parsley or garden cress

Butter the bread. Slice bread into 10 sections. Top each section with a lettuce leaf and a slice of liver paté. Garnish with chopped beets or gherkins and green herbs.

Cheese and Pear Sandwich
Smörgås med ost och päron

10 PORTIONS

1 tablespoon butter or margarine
5 slices of white bread
5 small leaves of lettuce
¼ lb. (100–150 g) blue cheese
2 well-ripened pears
½ lemon
1 finely sliced red pepper

Butter the bread and trim crusts. Slice the bread diagonally, making triangles. Top each slice with a lettuce leaf.

Mash the blue cheese with a fork. Slice the unpeeled pears lengthwise into slices about ¼ inch thick. Rub with lemon and put a slice of pear on each bread triangle. Top the pears with a spoonful of mashed blue cheese. Garnish with a thin slice of red pepper.

Smoked Meat Sandwich with Horseradish Dressing
Smörgås med rökt kött och pepparrotsgrädde

IO PORTIONS

1 tablespoon butter or margine
1 loaf of white or rye bread sliced lengthwise
10 small leaves of lettuce
½ cup (100–150 ml) whipping cream
1½–2 tablespoons grated horseradish
a little less than ¼ lb. (100 g) of thinly sliced reindeer
  or horse meat
salt

Butter the bread. Trim crusts and top with a slice of smoked meat. Cut the bread into rectangles or triangles. Place a lettuce leaf on each section. Whip cream and flavor with grated horseradish and salt. Put a small dollop of whipped cream on each lettuce leaf.

Smoked Fish and Scrambled Egg Sandwich
Smörgås med rökt fisk och äggröra

CA IO PORTIONS

1 loaf white bread sliced lengthwise
2 eggs
⅛ teaspoon salt
1 tablespoon butter or margarine
⅓ lb. (150 g) smoked eel, salmon, mackeral,
  or smoked Baltic herring
finely chopped fresh dill or chives

Trim crusts from bread. Beat eggs lightly and add salt.

Melt butter in saucepan. Turn egg mixture into saucepan. Cook slowly over low heat.

As eggs begin to set, lift with a spatula and turn gently. Allow the eggs to cool. Spread scrambled eggs evenly over the slice of bread and cut in rectangular sections.

Remove skin from fish and cut in slices. Divide evenly on the scrambled eggs and garnish with finely chopped dill or chives.

Sandwich Roll-Ups
Tunnbrödsrullar

4 PORTIONS

2–4 large rounds of soft flatbread
1 tablespoon soft margarine
SMOKED BALTIC HERRING FILLING:
3–4 smoked Baltic herrings
2 hard-boiled eggs
½ cup (50–100 ml) sour cream
¼ cup (50 ml) chopped parsely, chives or garden cress
HAM FILLING:
3–4 slices of lean cold boiled ham
1 cup (250 ml) cottage cheese
1 peeled apple
4–6 slices of medium sharp low-fat cheese
1 green or red sweet pepper, diced or finely sliced

Slice the rounds of flatbread halfwise. Butter bread lightly and choose either the smoked herring or ham filling.

Clean the herring well and tear the fillets in smaller pieces. Chop the eggs coarsely. Combine all ingredients in a small bowl, mixing well. Spread on bread sections. Roll the bread up and wrap in plastic wrap or aluminum foil. Tie a paper napkin around the sandwich roll.

Slice ham in slivers and mix with cottage cheese and a grated apple if desired. Spread mixture on half of each bread section. Cover the remaining half with cheese and diced peppers Roll the bread up and wrap in plastic wrap or aluminum foil. Tie a paper napkin around the sandwich roll.

Sandwich Cake with Shrimp and Roe

Sandwich Cake with Shrimp and Roe
Smörgåstårta med räkor och rom

IO PORTIONS

*1 large round loaf of white sandwich bread cut
lengthwise in 2 rounds*

FILLING:

*½ lb. (200 g) medium-sized shrimp, boiled , peeled,
and cleaned*

¼ cup (50 ml) finely chopped dill

½ cup (100 ml) mayonnaise

½ cup (100 ml) whipping cream

⅛ teaspoon paprika

GARNISH:

⅓ cup (50–100 ml) mayonnaise

1 bunch fresh dill

1 lemon

3 tablespoons large-grained red roe

*¼ lb. (100 g) medium-sized shrimp, boiled, peeled, and
cleaned*

Trim crusts if necessary. Chop shrimp and mix with
dill and mayonnaise. Whip cream and add to shrimp
mixture. Sprinkle with paprika. Spread half the filling
on one round of bread. Top with remaining bread
half and spread with remaining filling.

Frost sides of cake with mayonnaise. Garnish with
chopped dill. Save a few sprigs for decoration. Cut lemon in slices and cut lengthwise. Arrange attractively on cake. Divide the roe evenly on each lemon
slice. Garnish with shrimp and sprigs of fresh dill.

Salads

From once having been considered "rabbit food", salads have become a favorite dish in Sweden. Coleslaw is served as a sidedish at pizzerias. Towards the end of the 1960's, West Coast Salad, with shrimp and mussels, skyrocketed in popularity and was very often served on the party circuit. Chicken Salad, from the U.S.A., arrived on the scene a little later, as was the case for Cheese Salad which could be served together with red wine. Most definitely, salads are the improvisators salvation!

Tossed Green Salad
Blandad grönsallad

4 PORTIONS

½–1 head of bibb or boston lettuce
1 wedge isberg lettuce or chinese cabbage
3–4 leaves of endive
salad dressing:
1 tablespoon vinegar
   (or 1½ tablespoons of fresh lemon juice)
⅛ teaspoon salt
1 clove garlic, crushed
3 tablespooons vegetable oil
dash of white pepper

Rinse and clean the different salad greens under cold running water. Dry thoroughly. Rub a large salad bowl with a clove of garlic and tear or cut salad into bit-sized pieces, allowing the smaller greens to remain whole.

Finely slice the chinese cabbage.

DRESSING: Combine all ingredients in a small bowl or shaker. Allow garlic to draw awhile in dressing. Use a garlic press if stronger flavor is desired.

Put salad greens in a large bowl. Wait until just before serving to pour dressing on salad and toss gently. This is to avoid having the greens lose their crispness.

Swedish Coleslaw
Vitkålssallad med morot

Fresh green cabbage is available almost all year and makes a crispy salad. The shredded cabbage can easily be combined with many other fruits and vegetables as well.

4 PORTIONS

1 lb. (400 g) green cabbage
2 carrots
⅓ cup (100 ml) leeks, sliced in rings
DRESSING:
1 tablespoon fresh lemon juice
½ teaspoon salt
⅛ teaspoon pepper
2 tablespoons vegetable oil
1 tablespoon water

Rinse and clean vegetables. Shred cabbage finely and grate carrots coarsely. Use a food processor if available. Layer the ingredients in a salad bowl.

Mix together ingredients for dressing. Pour over salad or serve separately.

Tomato and Onion Salad
Tomatsallad med lök

4 PORTIONS

4–6 tomatoes
1 onion
1 tablespoon finely chopped parsley
DRESSING:
use Tossed Green Salad's dressing recipe (page 22)

Rinse tomatoes. Cut in thin slices and arrange in a serving dish. Peel onion. Chop f inely and sprinkle over tomatoes. Pour dressing over tomatoes and chill awhile. Sprinkle with chopped parsley just before serving.

Beet Salad with Lemon
Rödbetssallad med citron

Beet Salad goes well with boiled ham, brown sausage, and smoked or fried fish.

4 PORTIONS

6–10 fresh red beets
1 teaspoon salt per quart of water
onion, chopped
DRESSING:
use Tossed Green Salad's dressing recipe
   together with a little lemon (page 22)

Boil the beets approximately 20 minutes in lightly salted water.
   Slice the beets while still warm. Put them in a glass bowl. Sprinkle with finely chopped onion. Make salad dressing. Pour over the warm slices of beets and let cool before serving.

Cucumber Salad
Inlagd gurka (Pressgurka)

Cucumber salad is served as a complement to Swedish meatballs, for example.

4 PORTIONS

½ lb. (200 g) fresh european cucumbers
⅔ (150 ml) cup water
2 tablespoons vinegar essence (12 %)
2 tablespoons sugar
⅛ teaspoon salt
⅛ teaspoon white pepper
GARNISH:
2 tablespoons chopped parsley

Peel cucumber. Slice thin and put in a bowl. Make a marinade by mixing together the other ingredients. Pour over cucumbers and sprinkle with parsley.

Potato Salad
Potatissallad med majonnäs

This potato salad is often served with cold roast beef, smoked pork chops, ham, sausage, or smoked fish.

4 PORTIONS

8–10 firm medium-sized potatoes
½ cup (100 ml) finely sliced leeks
¼ cup (50 ml) chopped parsley or fresh dill
2 tablespoons capers
DRESSING:
½ cup (100 ml) sour cream
½ cup (100 ml) mayonnaise
1 teaspoon dried tarragon
salt, pepper
GARNISH:
radishes, chives

Scrub and boil potatoes. Drain and cool.
   Wash and finely slice the leek. Chop the parsley and dill. Slice or dice the potatoes. Put potatoes and chopped greens in salad bowl, alternating layers.
   Mix together ingredients for dressing . Pour over salad and fold in gently. Sprinkle with capers. Garnish with radishes and finely chopped chives before serving.

Red Cabbage, Apple, and Onion Salad
Rödkålssallad med äpple och lök

This colorful salad is often served with either fried or boiled sausage.

4 PORTIONS

¾ lb. (300 g) red cabbage
1 apple
¼ cup (50 ml) chopped chives or finely slivered leeks
DRESSING:
use Tossed Green Salad's dressing recipe (page 22)

Clean and shred cabbage finely. Core apple and cut in thin slices. Mix together all ingredients in a salad bowl. Make dressing and pour over salad or serve separately.

Smoked Herring Salad
Böcklingsallad

This salad can be served as a first course or as part of a smorgasbord.

4 PORTIONS

1¼ lb. (500–600 g) smoked Baltic herring
3 medium-sized potatoes
2 tart apples
¼ cup (50 ml) finely chopped chives"
DRESSING:
2 tablespoons vinegar
⅓ cup (75 ml) vegetable oil
⅛ teaspoon salt
dash of pepper
GARNISH:
1–2 tomatoes
lettuce leaves

Clean and fillet the herring. Tear fillets in smaller pieces. Dice apples and potatoes. Place herring in salad bowl and mix together with apples, potatoes, and chives. If one prefers, the herring, diced potatoes, and apples can be placed in separate sections in a shallow serving dish instead.

Combine ingredients for the dressing. Pour over salad, and garnish with lettuce and wedges of tomato.

Herring Salad
Sillsallad

Traditionally, Herring Salad is served as part of the Christmas smorgasbord.

4–6 PORTIONS

2 fillets of salt herring
3 boiled potatoes, cooled
1 whole pickle
1–2 tart apples
½–1 small onion
5 pickled beets
3 tablespoons beet juice
⅛ teaspoon white pepper
GARNISH:
2 hard-boiled eggs
4–5 springs of parsely
⅓ cup (100 ml) whipping cream (optional)

Soak fillets in cold water for 10–12 hours or according to directions on package.

Dice all the ingredients or chop in a food processor. Add beet juice, and season with salt and pepper. Chill for a few hours.

Transfer to a serving bowl and garnish with egg halves (or slices) and strips of chopped parsley. The salad can also be garnished with whipped cream.

Salmon Salad

Salmon Salad
Laxsallad

Salmon salad is served as an appetizer or a luncheon dish.

4 PORTIONS

¾ cup (200 ml) sour cream
¼ cup (50 ml) chili sauce
salad dressing (Tossed Green Salad's dressing recipe page 22)
2 teaspoons lemon juice
salt, pepper
8 medium-sized boiled potatoes
3–4 celery stalks

6–8 radishes
1 tablespoon chopped chives
¾ lb. (300 g) poached or smoked salmon
GARNISH:
lettuce leaves

Combine sour cream, chili sauce, salad dressing, and lemon juice. Season with salt and pepper.

Slice potatoes. Rinse celery and cut in fine strips. Wash and slice radishes. Line a salad bowl with lettuce leaves. Mix potatoes, celery, radishes, chives, and boned salmon cut in small pieces together and place in salad bowl. Serve dressing separately.

West Coast Salad
Västkustsallad

This salad can be made using only fresh shellfish. However, for a less elegant salad, frozen shellfish, or even canned, can be substituted.

4 PORTIONS

1 boiled lobster or crab
   or 8–12 Norwegian lobster tails (approximately
   ¼ lb./125 g if canned)
   or 15 cooked mussels (approximately ½ lb./250 g
   if canned)
¾ lb. (300 g) fresh shrimp, boiled and cleaned
½–⅔ cup (100–150 g) fresh mushrooms
½ cup (125 g) frozen peas
½ lb. (approximately 1 cup/300 g) canned asparagus spears
2 tomatoes
¼ lb. (100 g) wedge isberg lettuce

DRESSING:
2 tablespoons vinegar
¼ teaspoon pepper
½–1 clove garlic, pressed
4 tablespoons vegetable oil
2 tablespoons water

Thaw shellfish, if frozen. Drain, if canned. Split the lobster or crab in two, and remove meat from shellfish. Cut in good bite-sized pieces.

Mix the ingredients for the dressing and let the mixture draw awhile.

Wash, clean, and slice the mushrooms. Thaw the peas. Drain the can of asparagus.

Slice the tomatoes in wedges.

Shred the lettuce and spread out on a serving plate. Arrange the different salad components prettily in sections on the lettuce, or mix together in a large salad bowl.

Pour dressing on salad and chill before serving.

Serve toast and butter with the salad.

Shrimp Salad
Räksallad

Serve this salad as a first course together with rolls or toast.

4 PORTIONS

1¾ lb. (750 g) boiled shrimp, unpeeled
   (or approximately ½ lb./250 g peeled shrimp)
1 8 oz. can (½ lb./200 g) asparagus pieces
½ cup (125 g) frozen peas
¼ cup (50 g) fresh mushrooms
¼ lb. (100 g) wedge isberg lettuce

DRESSING:
½ (100 ml) cup mayonnaise
½ cup (100 ml) whipping cream
2 tablespoons chili sauce
1 tablespoon sherry
salt, pepper

Boil, cool, peel, and clean shrimp. If frozen and pre-cooked, thaw before peeling.

Drain asparagus. Thaw peas. Wash, clean, and slice mushrooms. Mix ingredients together.

Rinse and shred lettuce. Mix with other ingredients, or put in the bottom of a salad bowl.

Put salad in bowl. Mix mayonnaise and whipping cream for dressing. Add chili sauce and sherry. Season with salt and pepper if necessary. Drizzle dressing over salad or serve separately.

Chicken Salad
Kycklingsallad

Serve salad as a luncheon dish or evening meal together with homemade bread.

4 PORTIONS

1 fried or barbequed chicken
1 green pepper
4 tomatoes
½ cucumber
¼–½ head of isberg lettuce
¾ cup (200 ml) finely sliced celery

DRESSING:

1½ tablespoons fresh lemon juice or vinegar
⅛–¼ teaspoon dried tarragon
3 tablespoons vegetable oil
2 tablespoons water
salt, pepper

Bone the chicken, removing skin. Cut the meat in smaller pieces. Place them in the middle of a rather large serving plate.

Mix together the salad dressing. Season well with salt, pepper, and crushed tarragon leaves. Pour dressing over chicken. Chill 30–40 minutes in order to give flavor to the chicken. Baste several times.

Wash the green pepper, and slice in rings. Slice tomatoes in wedges, cucumber in sticks, and shred the lettuce. Arrange vegetables in sections around the chicken on the serving plate.

The salad dressing can be substituted with ½ cup mayonnaise and ½ cup sour cream or cream fraiche. Season with salt, pepper, celery salt, or curry.

Cheese and Radish Salad
Ostsallad med rädisor

Serve salad as a first course together with either boiled (or smoked) ham or toast.

4 PORTIONS

½ lb. (200 g) wedge of cheese, for example svecia, herrgård, or grevé
1–2 bunches of radishes
2–3 stalks of celery

DRESSING:

1 tablespoon vinegar
½ teaspoon salt
⅛ teaspoon pepper
2 tablespoons vegetable oil
½–1 tablespoon water

Dice cheese. Cut radishes in slices, and chop celery in smaller sections. Mix ingredients in a salad bowl.

Mix the salad dressing. Pour over salad just before serving.

Soups

At one time soup was considered to be a staple commodity in the Swedish household. Nowadays we don't dine on soup daily; however we don't want to miss the first nettle soup of spring, summers creamed vegetable soup made from the very first vegetables from the garden, and autumns hearty beef and vegetable soup with dumplings. Three classic Swedish soups well worth exporting – as are the other soups in this chapter!

Creamed Vegetable Soup
Ängamat

4 PORTIONS

1 head of cauliflower (approximately 1 lb.)
4–6 tender carrots
1 leek
¾ cup (200 ml) peas
3½ cups (800 ml) water
1 teaspoon salt
2 tablespoons flour
2 cups (400–500 ml) milk
2 tablespoons butter or margarine
½ teaspoon salt
⅛ teaspoon pepper
2 tablespoons finely chopped parsley

Rinse and clean vegetables. Divide the cauliflower into florets; cut the carrots into smaller pieces and cut the leek into thin slices.

Except for the leeks, boil vegetables almost 10 minutes or until tender. Add leeks to boiling water when vegetables are nearly cooked.

Mix together flour and water to a smooth paste. Add to boiling water together with margarine. Add remainder of milk. Let soup simmer a few minutes.

Season with salt and pepper. Sprinkle with parsley.

Nettle Soup
Nässelsoppa

In early spring Swedes like to go out in nature and pick tender young nettles. These make a fresh and fragile spring soup.

4 PORTIONS

8 cups (2 liter) tender young nettles
1 qt. (1 liter) beef bouillon (cubes + water)
2 tablespoons butter or margarine
3 tablespoons flour

Rinse nettles well. Place in saucepan. Add about 2 cups (500 ml) of water. Boil about 5–10 minutes. Strain. Chop nettles (Use food processor or osterizer if available).

Bring bouillon to boil. Add chopped nettles. Thicken soup with a paste of flour and margarine. Cook for about 3–5 minutes. Season and serve immediately.

Hard-boiled egg halves go nicely with nettle soup.

If frozen nettles are used, add the frozen block directly to the bouillon and bring to a boil.

The soup can be thickened after the nettles have thawed, and the soup has begun to boil.

Yellow Pea Soup
Gul ärtsoppa

This is absolutely one of the Swedish households most popular dishes. Moreover, it has a long history dating back to the Middle Ages. Traditionally, yellow pea soup and Swedish pancakes are eaten regularly on Thursdays.

4 PORTIONS

2½ cups (500 ml) quick-cooking dried yellow split peas
1½–2 qts. (1½–2 liter) water
½–1 tablespoon salt per quart of water
SOUP INGREDIENTS:
1¼ qt. (1¼ liter) water
½ teaspoon salt
1 small onion, peeled
2–3 whole cloves
½ lb. (250 g) lightly salted side pork or smoked shoulder butt
1 teaspoon majoram or thyme

Soak peas in salted water for 6–12 hours. Drain. The peas can be cooked without soaking but, in that case, must cook an extra hour. The best results are attained, however, by soaking the peas; one both shortens the cooking time as well as softens the hull of the peas.

Combine peas and water in a large sauce pot. Add salt, cover, and bring to a boil.

Skim the loose hulls and foam off the surface of the water.

Insert cloves into the peeled onion. Add onion to soup, together with pork in chunks. Simmer for approximately 1 hour.

Remove pork and allow to cool. Continue to simmer another 30 minutes. Remove onion.

Season with salt, majoram or thyme. Dilute with water if necessary.

Remove fat from pork and cut in cubes. Add to soup. The pork can also be sliced and served as a sidedish if desired.

Mushroom Soup
Svampsoppa

4–6 PORTIONS

1 qt. (1 liter) mixed variety of fresh mushrooms, washed and cleaned
or 1 cup (8 oz. can/200 g) mixed mushrooms or sliced champignons
2 tablespoons butter or margarine
⅓ cup (75 ml) flour
1½ qt. (1½ liter) bouillon (vegetable or chicken) plus liquid from mushrooms
½–¾ cup (100–200 ml) whipping cream
black pepper
worcestershire sauce
(salt)
(sherry)

Chop fresh mushrooms coarsley. Place in 5 qt. saucepan or kettle and allow mushrooms to sizzle on low heat until almost all liquid has evaporated. Add butter and continue to fry for a few minutes. Sprinkle with flour and mix. Dilute with bouillon and any additional liquid, strained, remaining from the mushrooms. If using canned mushrooms, strain and save liquid from can. Then prepare soup following the same recipe as for fresh mushrooms.

Add cream and season with salt, pepper , a dash of worcestershire sauce, and a little sherry if desired. Since bouillon can be salty, remember to be careful when adding salt to the soup.

Serve soup along with cheese sticks or crackers.

Kale Soup
Grönkålssoppa

Serve soup with chipolata or pork sausage, or finely sliced boiled ham. Kale soup can also be served together with lightly poached eggs.

4 PORTIONS

1 lb. (400–500 g) fresh kale (or equivalent if chopped and frozen)
2 tablespoons butter or margarine
3 tablespoons flour
1 qt. (1 liter) ham, pork, or beef bouillon
1–2 vegetable bouillon cubes
⅛–¼ teaspoon nutmeg
⅛–¼ teaspoon black pepper
(salt)
½ cup (100 ml) whipping cream

Rinse kale well and drain. Tear apart the leaves, removing the coarser stalks. Parboil kale and more tender stalks in lightly salted water about 10–15 minutes.

Strain water and chop the greens finely in a food processor or osterizer (Frozen kale only needs to be partially thawed).

Brown butter in a saucepan. Sprinkle with flour and dilute, little by little, with bouillon.

Add bouillon cubes as well as the chopped fresh (or partially thawed) kale. Bring to a boil and stir well. Season with nutmeg, black pepper, and salt, if necessary. Finally, round off by adding a little cream.

Spinach Soup
Spenatsoppa

Substitute 1 lb. fresh spinach (or ¾ lb. frozen, chopped spinach) for kale in the above recipe. Rinse fresh spinach well. Boil in lightly salted water in a large kettle for about 5 minutes. Strain. Chop spinach and then continue to follow the preceding recipe for Kale Soup.

Cabbage Soup from Skåne
Skånsk kålsoppa

4 PORTIONS

½ lb. (200–300 g) side of pork, bacon (or lightly cured pork shoulder)
1½ qt. (1½ liter) water
2–3 grains of allspice
¾ lb. (400 g) green cabbage
½ lb. (200 g) Swedish turnip (swede)
1–2 carrots
3–4 potatoes
GARNISH:
chopped parsley

Cut the meat in small cubes. The pork shoulder should be boned first , but the bone should be
boiled together with the meat. Put meat and bone in a sauce pot. Add water and bring to boil.
Skim and add allspice.
Wash, clean, and cut vegetables and potatoes in small cubes. Put in sauce pot and continue to simmer for 30 minutes or until everything is tender.
Remove bone and throw away. Sprinkle soup with parsley and serve as a main course.

Spinach Soup

Vegetable Beef Soup
Köttsoppa

Usually one chooses a boned cut of beef, such as brisket, ribs, shanks, or marrow, for this soup. These cuts give the broth a good hearty flavor. However, some boneless cuts of meat can also make a tasty soup.

4 PORTIONS

1 lb. (500 g) lean beef brisket
1½ qt. (1½ liter) water
1 teaspoon salt
5 white peppercorns
2–3 sprigs of parsley
1 bouillon cube
1 carrot
1 small parsnip
⅛ lb. (50 g) piece celeriac root
½ leek
parsley

Bring water to boil in a saucepan. Add meat, salt, peppercorns, parsley sprigs, and a bouillon cube, if desired. The bouillon cube isn't necessary, but it does give an additional accent to the broth. Simmer on low heat until meat is tender, approximately 1 hour.

Peel vegetables and wash the leek. Finely slice the carrot and parsnip in strips. Slice the leek in rings and dice the celeriac root. One can also use a food processor and grate everything coarsely.

Remove the cooked beef from the broth. Trim fat and cut in small sections. Strain broth into a saucepan. Add vegetables and meat. Simmer about 10–15 minutes until vegetables are almost tender. Add chopped parsley.

Serve piping hot, by all means, together with Swedish dumplings.

Dumplings
Klimp

4 PORTIONS

2 tablespoons butter or margarine
5 tablespoons flour
1 ¾ cups (400 ml) milk
2 egg yolks
salt, pepper
2–3 grated bitter almonds
(finely chopped parsley)

Melt butter in saucepan. Add flour and stir well. Add milk and bring to boil while stirring. Continue to boil for a few minutes. Remove from burner. Beat in egg yolks. Allow dough to simmer. Season with salt, pepper, and a little bitter almond, if desired.

Turn dough into a form or bowl rinsed in water. Allow to cool. Tip bowl upside down to release form. One can also drop the dumplings by rounded tablespoons into each bowl of soup. Sprinkle with parsley.

Black Soup with Liver Sausage
Svartsoppa

Black soup with liver sausage is so filling that it suffices as a main course by itself. It has a very spicy taste and is eaten piping hot. The giblets (neck, stomach muscle, and heart) are boiled separately in lightly salted water, cleaned, and cubed. Together with liver sausage (page 49), they are served as a sidedish.

8 PORTIONS

2 qts. (1 liter) bouillon
1 ⅔ cup (400 ml) goose or pig's blood
⅓ cup (75 ml) flour
½–1 tablespoon salt
3 tablespoons sugar
½ teaspoon white pepper
1 teaspoon ginger
1 teaspoon cloves
¾ cup (200 ml) juice from stewed apples and prunes
1–2 tablespoon vinegar
2–3 tablespoons cognac
½ cup (100 ml) port wine or sherry

Bring bouillon to boil. Make a paste of blood and flour. Add a little of the hot bouillon to blood mixture, beating vigorously. Pour blood mixture into rest of bouillon beating constantly. Simmer about 10 minutes beating steadily to prevent the soup from curdling.

Season with salt, pepper, sugar, spices, stew juice from fruit, vinegar, cognac, and wine.

The soup should have a strong flavor. Prepare it a day ahead of time if possible, allowing the spices time to draw.

Reheat soup carefully, beating steadily, just prior to serving.

Gourmet Shrimp Chowder
Fin räksoppa

4 PORTIONS

1 lb. (500 g) medium-sized boiled shrimp, unpeeled
1 onion, finely chopped
1 piece celeriac root (about 1/8 lb./50 g)
2 tablespoons butter or margarine
3 tablespoons flour
2 cups (500 ml) whipping cream
¾ cup (200 ml) fish bouillon
1¼ cups (300 ml) dry white wine
salt, pepper

Thaw shrimp, if frozen. Peel and put aside the peels from shrimp. Rinse shrimp quickly in cold water to prevent chowder from becoming too salty.

Cut the celeriac root into small pieces. Melt butter in large saucepan and brown onion and celeriac lightly. Towards the end, add peels from shrimp. Allow to sizzle a bit in saucepan.

Sprinkle with flour.

Add bouillon, cream, and wine. Cover tightly and simmer on low heat for 15 minutes.

Remove from heat. Strain shrimp peels from stock. Pour stock back into saucepan.

Dilute with bouillon or wine until consistency is satisfactory. Season with salt and pepper.

Reheat the chowder.

Warm the shrimp separately in a little bouillon or wine. Be careful not to let them boil. Add shrimp to chowder and serve immediately.

Meat

Mamma's Swedish meatballs, beef stew, roulades, and palace pot roast are all dishes that make Swedes, both at home and abroad, want to burst with patriotic pride! Swedes like to serve these foods which are an integral part of Swedish homecooking.

Swedish Meatballs
Köttbullar

"Mamma's meatballs" is a concept in Sweden, albeit there are as many versions of meatballs as there are mothers. They can either be large or small, served with or without gravy, seasoned with onions or allspice, and made from ground beef, ground pork, or a combination thereof. They are usually served as part of a smorgasbord or together with with boiled potatoes, vegetables, lingonberry jam, or sour pickles.

4 PORTIONS

BASIC GROUND MEAT RECIPE:
¼ cup (75 ml) oatmeal and 1 tablespoon potato flour
   or 4 tablespoons fine bread crumbs
¾ cup (200 ml) water
½–1 teaspoon salt
⅛ teaspoon pepper
1 lb. (400 g) ground meat (beef, pork, or a combination)
1 egg
FRYING:
1½ tablespoon butter or margarine
SAUCE:
2 tablespoons butter or margarine
2 tablespoons flour
1⅔ cups (400 ml) pan juice and dark bouillon
salt, pepper, soy sauce
(cream)

Mix together the oatmeal and potato flour or bread crumbs with the water. Stir in salt and pepper and set aside mixture to swell for 10 minutes. Work in the ground meat and the egg. Stir the ground meat mixture until smooth, being careful not to overstir. Overstirring causes the meat to become tough and stringy.

Roll meatballs to desired size and fry brown in but-ter or margarine. Keep them warm.

Melt the butter for the gravy in a saucepan. Add flour, while stirring, and let sizzle a bit. Remove from heat. Dilute with juice from pan or bouillon and stir until the mixture is smooth. Put saucepan back on burner and boil 3–5 minutes, stirring constantly. Add a little cream towards the end for a richer taste. Serve the sauce separately or place the meatballs in the sauce and warm thoroughly.

Beef Patties with Onions
Pannbiff med lök

4 PORTIONS

1 basic ground meat recipe
2 onions
FRYING:
3 tablespoons butter or margarine
¼ cup (75 ml) water

Mix the ground meat according to the meatball reci-pe and place on cutting board that has been rinsed in water. Make 12 beef patties. Melt a little butter in a frying pan and let sizzle a bit. Fry patties until nicely browned.

Cut the onions in thin slices. Fry in butter, marga-rine, or oil. Remove the onions, and finish frying the patties. Place them on a platter. Put the onions back in the pan. Pour water, over the onions, bring to a boil, and heat thoroughly. Pour the onions over the meat patties. Serve together with boiled potatoes and a green salad.

Swedish meatballs with mashed potatoes and cucumber salad (pages 34 and 23).

Biff à la Lindström
Biff Lindström

Mix the ground meat mixture together with ½ tablespoon or 2 tablespoons finely chopped pickled beets, the same proportions of onion as beets, and 1 teaspoon or 1 tablespoon capers. Shape into patties and fry. See Beef Patties, page 34.

Meatloaf
Köttfärslimpa

Meatloaf is baked in the oven and there exist many variations of this dish. It is served in slices with gravy or pan gravy, boiled potatoes, boiled vegetables or a salad, and lingonberry jam or sour pickles.

4 PORTIONS

1 basic ground meat recipe (see page 34)
1 tablespoon butter or margarine
water or bouillon
GRAVY:
1⅔ cups (400 ml) pan juice and bouillon
2 tablespoons flour
salt, pepper, soy sauce
⅓ cup (100 ml) cream

Mix the ground meat according to the meatball recipe. Grease an ovenproofed baking dish or small roasting pan. Shape the ground meat into a smooth loaf directly in the baking dish or pan.

Bake 45 minutes at 350°F (175°C). Brush with margarine a couple of times the last 10 minutes in the oven. Remove the meatloaf from the baking dish. Loosen the juice from the meatloaf in the baking pan by adding a little hot water or bouillon. Prepare the gravy. Dilute with water or bouillon to make 1⅔ cups (400 ml) gravy. Allow to boil 3–5 minutes. Season and add cream for a fuller flavor.

Swedish Stuffed Cabbage Rolls
Kåldolmar

4 PORTIONS

1 large head green cabbage (4 lbs./2 kg)
water
2 teaspoons salt per quart water
¼ cup (50 ml) long-grained rice
1 cup (200 ml) water
½ lb. (250 g) ground meat (combination pork and beef)
½–1 tablespoon salt
⅛ teaspoon pepper
FRYING:
1–2 tablespoons butter or margarine
bouillon or water from boiling cabbage
GRAVY:
1¼ cups (300 ml) pan gravy or bouillon
2 tablespoons arrowroot or potato flour
salt, pepper

Remove the large, outer leaves from the head of cabbage and parboil several minutes in boiling, salted water. Drain and cool.

In the meantime, boil the rice in the water and let cool. Mix the rice together with the ground meat, salt, and pepper to form a thin mixture. Divide evenly on the cabbage leaves and fold the cabbage leaves around the filling to form small packages.

Melt the fat in a frying pan and put the filled cabbage leaves, seamside down into the pan. Brown nicely all around and transfer cabbbage rolls to a pot or saucepan. Add some of the boiled cabbage water or bouillon to the frying pan and stir. Pour this pan gravy over the cabbage rolls. Cover and simmer about 30 minutes over low heat.

Measure the pan gravy and add bouillon. Make a paste with the arrowroot or potato flour and water and stir into the gravy. Bring to a boil and season with salt and pepper.

Serve the cabbage rolls in their own gravy together with boiled or mashed potatoes. Lingonberry or cranberry jam makes a refreshing complement to cabbage rolls.

Steak Smothered in Onions
Biff med lök

A Swedish classic that must be served at once and preferably together with new boiled potatoes and a green salad.

4 PORTIONS

4–5 onions
2 tablespoons butter, margarine, or oil
⅓ cup (100 ml) water
⅛ teaspoon salt
4 slices of top round or sirloin steak, ½" thick
½–1 teaspoon salt
1–2 pinches pepper

Cut the onion in thin slices. Melt the butter in a frying pan, allowing it foam and get color. Add the onion, stir, and reduce heat. Sauté the onion on low heat until golden yellow in color. Add the water and salt, and keep the onion warm.

Fry the steaks. For medium rare steaks, allow 2 minutes on each side and 3–4 minutes on each side if they are to be well done. Season with salt and pepper.

Put the steaks on a serving platter and pour hot onions over top.

Fried Pork with Onion Sauce
Stekt fläsk med löksås

4 PORTIONS

¾ lb. (400 g) lightly salted side of pork
SAUCE:
2 tablespoons butter or margarine
2 finely chopped onions
2 cups (450–500 ml) milk
⅛ teaspoon salt
⅛ teaspoon white pepper

Cut the rind from the pork. Slice in smaller pieces if necessary. Place the pork in a cold frying pan and place over heat. Reduce the heat when the fat begins to render. Fry 2–3 minutes on each side, depending on how crisp you would like the pork.

Melt the butter in a saucepan over low heat. Sauté the onion in the fat. Remove saucepan from burner. Stir in the flour. Add all the milk at once. Replace on burner and bring to a boil, stirring constantly. Boil 3–5 minutes. Season with salt and pepper.

Boiled Falu Sausage with Horseradish Sauce
Kokt falukorv med pepparrotssås

4 PORTIONS

¾ lb. (400 g) Falu sausage
1½ cups (300–400 ml) water
1 bouillon cube
3 slices onion
2 sprigs parsley
SAUCE:
2 tablespoons butter or margarine
2 tablespoons flour
1⅓ cups (300 ml) milk
¼–⅓ cup (50–100 ml) water from boiling the sausage
grated horseradish
(salt and pepper)

Remove the skin from the sausage. Place whole or sliced sausage in a saucepan. Add the water and bouillon cube (It gives the sausage a hearty flavor). Add the onion and parsley. Allow the sausage to simmer until thoroughly heated.

Heat the butter and flour for the sauce. Dilute with the boiled water from cooking the sausage and milk and allow to boil. Add the grated horseradish and salt and pepper to taste.

Serve with boiled potatoes and a cabbage salad.

Roulades of Beef
Oxrulader

4 PORTIONS

1⅓ lbs. (600 g) thinly sliced round steak or sirloin
1 teaspoon salt
⅛ teaspoon pepper
FILLING 1:
4 slices bacon
FILLING 2:
6 brisling anchovy style (Swedish anchovy fillets)
3 tablespoons chopped onion
FILLING 3:
4 tablespoons blue cheese
FRYING:
2 tablespoons butter, margarine, or oil
1½ cups (300–400 ml) water
SAUCE:
1⅓ cups pan (300 ml) juice and/or bouillon
2 tablespoons flour
⅓ cup (100 ml) cream
soy sauce, pepper, salt

Put slices of meat on a chopping board. Sprinkle with salt and pepper. Place one of the fillings on the meat slices. Roll together, securing with a toothpick.

Melt butter in a sauté pan and brown the roulades all around. Dilute with water. Cover, and let braise over low heat until tender, about 45 minutes. Remove the meat from the pan and remove toothpicks. Keep the roulades warm.

Thicken the pan juice with the flour to make a sauce. Add cream and season with soy sauce, pepper, and salt. Pour the sauce over the roulades.

Serve the roulades together with potatoes and boiled vegetables.

Swedish Hash
Pytt i panna

The classic Swedish "pytt i panna" is made from finely diced meat, potatoes, and onion. Adding smoked bacon or ham to the meat gives the dish an extra flavor.

4–6 PORTIONS

9–12 cold, boiled potatoes
1¼ cups (300 g) fried or boiled meat or sausage
2 onions
1 teaspoon salt
⅛ teaspoon pepper
¼ cup (50 ml) parsley
FRYING:
2 tablespoons butter, margarine, or oil

Dice the peeled potatoes and meat or sausage. Finely chop the onion.

Fry the potatoes and onion in a large frying pan. Brown the meat and sausage separately. Blend the ingredients together in the frying pan. Heat carefully. Salt and pepper. Sprinkle with finely chopped parsley.

Pot Roast of Beef in Cider
Ciderkokt kött

4–6 PORTIONS

2 lbs. (1 kg) chuck roast (approximately)
16 oz. (1,2 liter) cider (or applejuice)
2 slices of lemon
1 tablespoon dried mint
½ tablespoon salt
5–6 white peppercorns
SAUCE:
1¾ cups (400 ml) bouillon
2 tablespoons flour
salt, pepper

Put cider, lemon, mint, salt, and pepper in a large saucepot or Dutch oven. Insert a meat thermometer into the thickest part of the meat. The cider should cover the meat. If it doesn't, add a little water. Cover

Swedish Hash

and simmer over low heat until the thermometer reaches 185–195°F (85–90°C), approximately 1–1½ hours.

Remove the pot from the burner and let rest, covered, for 20 minutes. The meat will then finish cooking at the correct temperature.

Remove the meat from the pot. Strain the bouillon. Stir 1¾ cups bouillon together with 2 tablespoons flour, mixed with a little water. Salt and pepper to taste.

Serve the meat in slices, together with the sauce, potatoes, and boiled vegetables.

Veal in Dill Sauce
Dillkött

4 PORTIONS

2 qts. (2 liter) water
2 lbs. (1 kg) veal brisket, shoulder, back, or breast
1 tablespoon salt
½ teaspoon white peppercorns
2 onions
3 whole cloves
SAUCE:
2 tablespoons butter or margarine
2 tablespoons flour
1⅔ cups (400 ml) bouillon
(salt, pepper)
1–2 egg yolks
2 tablespoons cream
3 tablespoons fresh dill
½ tablespoon vinegar
⅛ teaspoon sugar

Measure the water and then bring to a boil.

Remove excess fat from veal and place tightly in a saucepan. Pour the water over the meat. Bring to a boil. Skim. Add salt, white peppercorns , onion, and cloves. Cover and simmer over low heat 1–1½ hours, the time depending on the quality of the meat. Prick with cake tester to see if the meat is soft inside. Remove from heat when tender. Let stand, covered, about 20 minutes.

Remove meat from saucepan and slice into equal pieces. Keep warm.

Prepare the sauce. Melt butter or margarine in a saucepan. Add flour and let sizzle while stirring. Dilute with the bouillon and stir until smooth. Remove from heat and let cool a bit. Beat in cream mixed with egg yolks and let sauce simmer. It must not boil. Season with salt and pepper and flavor with the dill, vinegar, and sugar.

Serve the veal in the sauce together with boiled potatoes or rice and a cabbage salad.

Swedish Beef Stew
Kalops

Everyday cooking at its best, perfect for a cold winter day.

4–6 PORTIONS

2 lbs. (1 kg) chuck roast or top round
2 tablespoons butter, margarine, or oil
2 onions
3 tablespoons all-purpose flour
1½–1¾ cups (300–400 ml) water
1 tablespoon salt
10 whole allspice
2 bay leaves

Cut up the meat in large cubes and brown in butter, margarine, or oil in a sauté pan. Slice the onion in wedges and brown a few minutes together with the meat.

Sprinkle with flour, stir well, and dilute with water. Add salt and spices. Cover and braise over low heat until the meat is tender and loosens from the bone. This should take about 1–1½ hours, depending on the quality of the meat. Stir occasionally to keep meat from sticking to the bottom of the pan. Add more water if the sauce is too thick.

Serve together with potatoes, lingonberries or pickled beets, and a green cabbage salad.

Veal in Dill Sauce

Sailor's Beef
Sjömansbiff

Meat, sauce, and potatoes in the same casserole make this an ideal meal at sea. It is a dish that has become a Swedish classic.

4 PORTIONS

1 lb. (500 g) ½" thick slices of boneless beef
3 onions
2 tablespoons butter, margarine, or oil
¾ cup (200 ml) water
12 potatoes
2 teaspoons salt
¼ teaspoon pepper
8 oz. (33 cl) dark beer or bouillon
parsley

Slice the meat into smaller pieces, if necessary. Peel and slice the onion. Sauté in one-third of the margarine over medium heat in a frying pan until it has a good color. Remove and set aside. Brown meat in rest of the margarine. Remove from the pan. Pour off the fat and stir a little hot water into the frying pan to loosen the juice from the meat in the pan. Save. Peel and slice potatoes. Place potatoes, onions, and meat in a baking dish or casserole in alternating layers. See that both the bottom and top layers are potatoes. Season each layer with salt and pepper.

Pour juice from the meat as well as the beer or bouillon over the layers. Cover and let simmer over low heat for 45 minutes or in 375°F (200°C) oven. Sprinkle with chopped parsley before serving. Serve together with a green salad and pickled gherkins or beets.

Porter Roast
Porterstek

4 PORTIONS

2 lbs. (1 kg) chuck roast
8 oz. (33 cl) bottle Porter or other dark beer
¼–½ cup (50–100 ml) black currant juice concentrate or 8–10 black currant leaves
½ cup (100 ml) Chinese soy sauce
1 teaspoon thyme
5–6 black peppercorns
2–3 bouillon cubes
(2 crushed cloves garlic)
1 large onion, in wedges
GRAVY:
1¾ cups (400 ml) broth
2½ tablespoons all-purpose flour
⅓ cup (100 ml) cream

Bind the meat together if necessary.

Blend together all the other ingredients in a saucepot, making sure the pot has room for a meat thermometer. Bring to a boil. Place the meat in the pot and braise over low heat about 45 minutes.

Insert the thermometer, deep into the thickest part of the meat and continue to cook until the thermometer shows 160°F (75°C), about 1–1½ hours.

Remove the pot from the heat and let meat rest in its broth about 20 minutes before starting to carve.

Strain the broth. Beat flour and cream together until thick. Beat into broth. Let boil several minutes.

Serve the meat in thin slices together with the gravy, boiled potatoes, and vegetables.

Palace Pot Roast
Slottsstek

8–10 PORTIONS

3 lbs. (1 ½ kg) boneless beef, rump roast, or tender
    shoulder
2 tablespoons butter or margarine
2–3 red onions
1–1½ teaspoons salt
12 white or black peppercorns
6 whole allspice
1 bay leaf
6–8 brisling, anchovy style (Swedish anchovy fillets)
2 cups (500 ml) water
GRAVY:
1½ cups (300–400 ml) strained pan juice
1½–2 teaspoons vinegar essence (12%)
2–3 tablespoons light corn syrup
2–3 tablespoons all-purpose flour
½–¾ cup (100–200 ml) cream
1–2 tablespoons Chinese soy sauce
½–1 teaspoon Worcestershire sauce

Trim the meat. Dry with paper towel.

Melt the margarine in a Dutch oven or saucepot and wait until the foam disappears before placing the meat, serving side down, into the pot. Brown slowly on all sides on low-medium heat. Insert a meat thermometer.

Add the peeled and sliced onions. Salt the meat and place the other spices, vinegar essence, syrup, and anchovies next to the meat.

Reduce the heat. Add the water. Cover and braise to 160°F (75°C), or 45 minutes per pound of meat.

Remove the meat and wrap in aluminum foil. Let rest for 15 minutes.

Make the gravy. Strain and measure the juice from the pan. Pour into saucepan. Thicken with flour dissolved in cold water and bring to a fast boil. Boil 2–3 minutes, making certain the gravy doesn't scorch the bottom of the pot..

Reduce the heat and beat in cream, soy sauce, and worcestershire sauce. Season carefully.

Carve the meat in thin, even slices. Place on serving platter and serve with boiled vegetables, potatoes, and gravy in a separate bowl.

Roast of Veal
Kalvstek

4–5 PORTIONS

2–3 lbs. (1–1½ kg) veal joint with bone or 1–1½ lbs.
    (600–700 g) boneless roast
1 tablespoon salt
⅛ teaspoon white pepper
1 teaspoon rosemary or sage
CREAM GRAVY:
1 tablespoon butter or margarine
2 tablespoons flour
1½ cups (300–400 ml) pan juice + bouillon
⅔ cup (100–200 ml) cream
grated whey-cheese or currant jelly

Rub the meat with salt, pepper, and rosemary or sage. Insert a meat thermometer into the thickest part of the roast. Place the meat in a baking pan of appropriate size. Roast on a rack in the lower part of the oven at 350°F (175°C) until the thermometer shows 160–175°F (70–75°C), depending on whether or not the roast should be medium or well done. Allow 1¼–1½ hours for roasting..

Dilute the pan juice with a little water. Brown a little margarine for the gravy. Add flour and stir. Dilute with pan juice from the roast, bouillon, and cream until right consistency. Add cheese or currant jelly for flavor.

Serve the meat in thin slices together with boiled potatoes, vegetables, gravy, pickles and/or jelly or lingonberry jam.

Roasted Loin of Pork
Ugnsstekt fläskkarré

4 PORTIONS

1¾–2 lbs. (800 g–1 kg) pork loin or loin chops on the bone
    or 1–2 lbs. (600–800 g) boneless pork loin or chops
1 teaspoon salt
⅛ teaspoon black pepper
½–1 teaspoon ground ginger
1 teaspoon rosemary or sage
GRAVY:
1¼ cups (300 ml) juice from the baking pan + water
    or bouillon
1–1½ teaspoons arrowroot
salt, pepper
(herb salt)

Trim the meat. Roll the boneless pork loin and bind to ensure an even shape. Mix together the salt, pepper, ginger, and herbs and rub into the roast.

Insert a meat thermometer into the thickest part of the meat, being certain that the thermometer doesn't touch the bone.

Place the meat in an ovenproofed baking dish or shallow roasting pan. Roast on a rack in lower part of the oven at 350°F (175°C) until thermometer shows 195°F (85°C) or 1½–2 hours, depending on size of meat and whether or not the meat is boned. Remove, wrap in foil, and allow to rest 15 minutes.

Stir a little hot water or bouillon into the pan juice. Measure and pour into a saucepan.

Thicken the pan juice with flour which has been dissolved in cold water and bring to a boil. Season with salt, pepper and optional herbs.

Bone the roast using a sharp narrow knife. Start from the backside and work downwards toward the base of the backbone. Turn the roast on its side and carve close to the ribs. Slice the meat in thin, even slices and place on a warm serving platter.

Serve together with hot vegetables, potatoes, and gravy.

Polar Roast
Tjälknöl

10 PORTIONS

2–3 lbs. (1–1½ kg) frozen roast beef or moose joint
SALT SOLUTION:
1 qt. (1 liter) water
⅓ cup (100 ml) salt
1 tablespoon sugar
½ teaspoon crushed black peppercorns
5–6 crushed juniper berries
1 crumbled bay leaf

Place the frozen meat in a shallow roasting pan. Roast 10–12 hours at 165°F (75°C). Insert a meat thermometer in the thickest part of the roast after 2–3 hours when the roast has thawed a bit. The meat is rare when the thermometer reaches 140°F (60°C), medium rare at 165°F (75°C), and well done at 175°F (80°C).

Mix the water, salt, sugar, and spices together and bring to a boil. Let cool.

Place the warm roast in the salt solution and let stand in a cool place for 4–5 hours. The roast should not soak longer or it will become too salty.

Serve with baked potatoes or potatoes au gratin and a nice salad.

Saddle of Reindeer
Rensadel

Fresh saddle is usually only found in specialty shops, but most supermarkets stock frozen roasts which can be prepared without thawing. In that case, the roasting time is longer and a lower oven temperature is used.

6–8 PORTIONS

3–4 lbs. (1½–2 kg) saddle of reindeer
1½–2 teaspoons salt
2–3 pinches white pepper
lard
bouillon or water

SAUCE:

1½–2 cups (400–500 ml) pan juice and bouillon
4 tablespoons flour
⅓ cup (100 ml) cream
salt, pepper
(black currant jelly)
(madeira)

Using a sharp knife, remove the shiny white membranes from the top of the saddle before preparation. Otherwise, the meat will shrink together. If the roast is frozen, thaw in room temperature until the membranes can be pulled off carefully.

Rub the saddle with salt and pepper.

Since the meat is very lean, the roast needs to be covered with thin slices of lard to prevent it from drying out. Drive a skewer through the backbone of the saddle to help it keep its form while roasting.

Place the meat on a rack in a roasting pan. Line the pan with aluminum foil to make it easier to collect the juices from the pan after roasting. Place a meat thermometer in the roast, making certain that its point doesn't touch a bone. Roast at 350°F (175°C) if fresh and 300°F (150°C) if frozen. When the thermometer shows 160°F (75°C), the meat is rosy inside.

It is well done when the temperature reaches 170°F (80°C). Calculated roasting time is 45 minutes for fresh meat and 1½ hours for frozen.

Remove from oven when done and cover with aluminum foil and let rest until time to carve.

Meanwhile, prepare the gravy. Stir a little hot water or bouillon into the roasting pan to dissolve the pan drippings. Strain liquid and measure. Add more bouillon if necessary. Thicken the gravy with flour. Add a little cream. Season well with salt, pepper, and optional madeira.

Carve and serve. Serve saddle of reindeer together with oven-fried potatoes (for example, Hasselback potatoes), jelly made from the berries of the mountain ash tree, string beans and/or cherry tomatoes and a green salad.

Reindeer Stew
Rengryta

Fresh reindeer meat is found mainly in Northern Sweden. In the rest of the country, fresh reindeer is limited to specialty stores, although most supermarkets do carry frozen reindeer meat. Thaw the frozen reindeer meat so that the pieces can be separated before preparation.

4 PORTIONS

1 ⅓ lbs. (600 g) boneless reindeer meat, flank or shoulder
2 tablespoons butter or margarine
¾ tablespoon all-purpose flour
1 teaspoon salt
⅛ teaspoon pepper
¾ teaspoon whole dried juniper berries
1 cup (200–250 ml) bouillon
1 qt. (¾–1 liter) fresh chantarelle mushrooms
1 tablespoon butter or margarine

Cut the meat into pieces and brown in a Dutch oven or sauté pan.

Sprinkle with the flour, salt, and freshly-ground pepper. Stir well. Add the juniper berries. Dilute with the bouillon, cover, and braise meat over low heat until tender. This takes about an hour, depending on the quality of the meat.

Clean the mushrooms and slice into large pieces. Sauté lightly in the butter. Add to stew and season to taste.

Serve the stew hot together with potatoes, jelly, sour pickles, and green salad.

Rabbit, venison, roebuck, deer, or moose may be substituted for the reindeer.

Fresh mushrooms can be substituted with either canned mushrooms or frozen vegetables.

Roast Goose
Stekt gås

Goose is traditionally served in Skåne on "Mårten Gås", November 11th, together with boiled apple halves, stewed prunes, boiled or fried potatoes, red cabbage or brussel sprouts, and gravy.

8–10 PORTIONS

1 goose (10–12 lbs./5 kg)
1 lemon
3 teaspoons salt
1 teaspoon white pepper
STUFFING:
4 apples, peeled
1 cup (200 g) prunes
bouillon and stew juice
GRAVY:
2 cups (500 ml) pan drippings
1–1½ tablespoons arrowroot or potato flour,
*   or 2½ tablespoons all-purpose flour*
salt, white pepper

Thaw the goose if frozen.

Boil the neck, wings, gizzards, and heart in lightly salted water together with a few white peppercorns, 1 sprig parsley, and 1 slice of onion to make a hearty bouillon. Save to use for the gravy. The liver can be fried separately.

Rub the inside of the goose with lemon and then with a little salt and pepper. Stuff with thick slices of peeled apples and pitted prunes. Truss goose and place breast side up in a roasting pan. Rub the outside with salt and pepper. Place in lower part of oven and roast at 350°F (175°C) for 2½–3 hours. Baste occasionally.

For a crisp and shiny skin pour several tablespoons of cold water over the goose and leave the oven door ajar the last 15 minutes of roasting.

To test for doneness insert a needle into the thigh. If the needle goes in easily and the juice running out from the puncture is clear, the goose is ready. Remove from oven.

Allow to rest before carving.

Stir a little bouillon and juice from stewed prunes into the roasting pan. Strain and measure the juice and skim fat from the surface. Blend the flour in a little cold water and pour into the hot drippings in an even stream. Barely bring the gravy to a quick boil if arrowroot or potato flour is used. If flour is used, boil 3–5 minutes. Salt and pepper to taste. Carve the goose.

Spareribs
Revbensspjäll

In Southern Sweden pigs have always been butchered so that spareribs were cut thick. Before, it was the custom to cook spareribs on the stove in a big kettle; however oven-baked spareribs are more common today. They are both easier to prepare and more succulent.

4 PORTIONS

2½ lbs. (1 kg) thick-cut, "country style", spareribs
1 teaspoon salt
1½ pinch pepper
¼ teaspoon ginger
hot water

Rub the ribs with salt and spices. Place fat side up in a roasting pan. Roast 1½ hours at 350°F (175°C).

Remove the ribs from the pan. Skim excess fat from pan drippings and add a little hot water to the drippings to make pan gravy. Slice the meat.

Serve with boiled potatoes and red cabbage or brussels sprouts, stewed prunes, and applesauce.

Christmas Ham

Christmas Ham
Julskinka

Most Swedes serve ham at Christmas. It can be baked, boiled, or bought already pre-cooked. A broiled glaze made from mustard and bread crumbs makes the Christmas ham complete. The ham should weigh at least 5 pounds if it is going to to be baked. The ham is served at the Christmas smorgasbord together with mustard, applesauce, and red cabbage.

---

1 ham 5–15 lb. (2–6 kg) lightly salted, bone-in or
  boneless
BROILED GLAZE: (FOR A 7 ½ LB. HAM)
1 egg
3 tablespoons mustard
1 teaspoon sugar
2–3 tablespoons fine dried bread crumbs

Quickly rinse the ham in cold water. Wrap in aluminum foil. Insert a meat thermometer into the thickest part of the ham. Place on a rack in a roasting pan. Bake in oven until thermometer shows 165°F (75°C). Allow 25–40 minutes per pound. Remove the ham from the oven and loosen the rind.

Place the ham on a rack in a roasting pan.

Mix together the egg, mustard, and sugar to make a glaze. Coat the ham with the glaze. Sprinkle bread crumbs on top. Place in oven set at 400°F (200°C) and broil until golden brown.

Jellied Veal
Kalvsylta

Jellied veal is a Christmas dish and a traditional part of the Swedish smorgasbord. It can also be served, however, independently as a main course together with boiled or fried potatoes and pickled beets. This jellied veal is made with ground, boiled veal.

2½–3 LBS. JELLIED VEAL

3 lbs. (1½ kg) back or shank of veal
water
1 tablespoon salt per quart water
1 bay leaf
1 teaspoon white peppercorns
1 onion

Place the meat in a kettle. Measure the water and pour in kettle until the meat is just barely covered. Add salt. Bring to a boil and skim. Add spices and peeled onion. Cover and let simmer over low heat until the meat is tender and loosens from the bone, about 1½ hours.

Allow the meat to cool slightly. Remove from kettle and strain the broth. Rinse the kettle out with water. Pour the strained bouillon back into the kettle, bring to a boil, and reduce a little.

Grind the meat using a coarse grinding blade or dice as evenly as possible. Place the meat in the bouillon and bring to a boil. Season.

Pour the mixture into forms that have been rinsed in water and let stand in a cool place until firm.

If desired, substitute with equal parts of pork and veal shanks. Follow the recipe above. That latter variation is less expensive, but also contains more fat.

Liver Paté
Leverpastej

Liver paté is associated with Christmas and the smorgasbord.

ABOUT 2½ LBS. (1 KG)

1½ tablespoons butter or margarine
¼ cup (75 ml) flour
1½ cups (350 ml) milk
½ lb. (250 g) lard
1 lb. (500 g) pig's or calve's liver
1 anchovy fillet
1 onion
½ tablespoon butter or margarine
1 egg
¾ tablespoon salt
3 pinches white pepper
¼ teaspoon cloves
slices of lard to line baking dish

Melt the butter in a saucepan. Add flour and dilute with milk until sauce is thick. Simmer 3–5 minutes.

Grind the lard and stir into the warm sauce. Allow to stand until the lard melts.

Grind the liver twice: once using a coarse blade or plate and then once again using a fine. Add the anchovy fillet to the second grinding.

Peel and finely chop the onion. Brown lightly. (Instead of chopping and browning the onion, it can also be included in the second grinding).

Cool the mixture after the lard has melted. Add the ground liver, onion, egg, salt, and spices.

Grease or line a 1½ qt. bread pan with thin slices of lard. Pour the liver paté mixture into the form and cover with aluminum foil.

Bake in a water-bath in the oven at 350°F (175°C) for one hour. Allow to cool before removing from form.

Pork Sausage
Fläskkorv

Pork sausage is served together with mashed potatoes, mashed turnips, or red cabbage.

11–13 LBS. SAUSAGE

3 lbs. (1½ kg) potatoes
3 cups (750 ml) milk
2½ lbs. (1 kg) boneless beef
2½ lbs. (1 kg) lean pork
2½ lbs. (1 kg) lard
3 tablespoons salt
½ tablespoon ginger

½ tablespoon allspice
½ tablespoon white pepper
3 cups (750 ml) bouillon
about 15 feet (5 m) sausage casing
SALT MIXTURE FOR RUBBING THE CASINGS:
2½ tablespoons salt
1 teaspoon saltpeter
1 tablespoon sugar
FOR BOILING:
5 whole allspice
1 bay leaf
1 teaspoon salt per quart of water

Check that the sausage casings are whole. Boil the potatoes and milk separately. Chill well.

Grind the meat twice in a food processor or 3–4 times through a regular food grinder. Grind the lard and potatoes once. (If a food processor is being used, be sure to weigh the ground meat, lard, and potatoes so that the individual batches have the right proportions and are suitable in size for the machine.)

Begin by blending both the ground meats together with the lard in a large mixing bowl. Add potatoes and spices and dilute with milk and bouillon, a little at a time, at the same time.

Work the entire mixture 45 minutes by hand or 15 minutes for each batch mixed in a food processor. Mix together all the separate batches mixed by the food processor. Boil or fry a sample to taste.

Stuff the sausage mixture into the casings, being careful not to overstuff. Tie off the casings at intervals that are sausage length. Cool the sausages and rub with the salt mixture. Cool in the refrigerator for several hours.

The sausages can either be boiled or frozen.

To boil, place the sausages in a large saucepot. Add just enough water to cover the sausages. Add spices and salt. Simmer, uncovered, for about 30 minutes, being careful not to let the sausage boil. Using a couple of large spoons, turn the sausage over once while cooking.

Liver Sausage
Leverkorv

Liver sausage, together with Black Soup, is the traditional food served on St. Martin's Day.

8 PORTIONS

1 lb. (400 g) calf or chicken livers
2 cups (500 ml) milk
⅓ cup (75 ml) rice
3 tablespoons finely chopped onion
3 tablespoons butter or margarine
¼ lb. (100 g) ground pork
1 egg
½ cup (100 ml) raisins
1½–2 teaspoons salt
¼ teaspoon white pepper
1 teaspoon majoram
1 (teaspoon potato flour)
½ yard (½ m) sausage casing

Grind or finely chop the liver. Thaw first, if frozen. Bring milk to boil and add rice. Let rice cook on low heat until soft. Cool.

Brown onion lightly in melted butter, avoiding the onion from turning color.

Mix liver with rice, onion, ground meat, eggs, raisins, salt, and spices. Test by frying a little piece of sausage filling. Add a little potato flour if filling is runny. If filling is bland, add more salt and spices .

Stuff the sausage loosely in the casing. Tie off in knots in a few places.

Put sausage in warm, lightly salted water, and simmer for about 30 minutes.

Slice sausage and serve cold together with Black Soup.

Fish

Sweden's long coastline and many lakes furnish it with an abundance of fish and an almost incredible variety of recipes. It's been difficult to sort and choose the content of this chapter! Try the herring recipes and Jansson's Temptation. You can't miss!

Pickled Herring
Inlagd sill

Pickled herring is a prerequisite of the Swedish smorgasbord, but can also be served alone with fresh new potatoes and, sometimes, sour cream. The herring must soak in water at least 10–12 hours prior to preparation.

4 PORTIONS

2 salted Iceland herring or 4 salt herring fillets
   (1 lb./420 g)
1–2 red onions
PICKLING SOLUTION:
1 cup (200 ml) water
½ cup (100 ml) vinegar essence (12 %)
⅔ cup (150–175 ml) sugar
10 whole allspice berries
5 white peppercorns
1 bay leaf

Gut the Iceland herring and let soak in plenty of water for 24 hours. Soak the herring fillets for 10–12 hours or follow instructions on the can.

Skin and fillet the whole herring. Slice the fillets into ⅓" (1½ cm) thick pieces.

Peel the onions and slice thin.

Blend together the ingredients for the pickling solution. Bring to a boil and then allow to cool.

Put the herring and onions in a jar in alternating layers. Pour the pickling solution over the herring. It is ready to serve after 3–4 hours, but tastes better if allowed to stand at least 24 hours. Store in cool place.

Glazier's Herring
Glasmästarsill

This is also one of the components of the smorgasbord and is always found on the Christmas smorgasbord.

4 PORTIONS

2 salted Iceland herring (about 1⅓ lbs.)
PICKLING SOLUTION:
¾–1 cup (150–200 ml) sugar
½ cup (100 ml) vinegar essence
1 cup (200 ml) water
1 bay leaf
5 whole allspice berries
½ carrot, sliced
1 red onion, sliced
1 piece horseradish, finely diced

Gut the herring, allowing the skin and backbone to remain. Soak in plenty of water for 24 hours.

Cut the herring crosswise in ¾" (2 cm) slices.

Mix together a solution of sugar, vinegar essence, water, bay leaf, and allspice. Bring to a boil and then allow to cool.

Put the herring and vegetables in a jar in alternating layers, and pour the cooled solution over the herring, ensuring its completely covered. Refrigerate 24 hours before serving.

Jars of Glazier's herring and raw pickled Baltic herring with Brogård's bread in the background (recipe page 90).

Herring in Mustard Sauce
Senapssill

2 salted Iceland herring fillets (about 1¼ lbs./600 g) or
1 lb. can (16 oz./420 g) salt herring that has been
pre-soaked in water.
PICKLING SOLUTION:
2 cups (500 ml) water
½ cup (100 ml) vinegar essence (12 %)
¼ cup (50 ml) sugar
SAUCE:
¾ cup (200 ml) mustard
4 tablespoons sugar
2 tablespoons vinegar
4 tablespoons vegetable cooking oil
¼ cup (50 ml) finely chopped dill

Gut the Iceland herring and let soak in plenty of water for 24 hours. Soak the salt herring fillets in water for 10–12 hours.

Rinse the fillets well. Skin and fillet the whole herring. Blend together the ingredients for the pickling solution and pour over the fillets. Let stand in a cool place for one hour.

Take the fillets and slice into smaller pieces. Mix ingredients for the sauce. Place the herring in a glass jar and pour the mustard sauce over the fish. Chill 24 hours before serving.

Sun's Eye
Sölöga

This is a traditional Easter dish.

4 PORTIONS

1–2 onions
5–6 pickled beets
2 tablespoons capers
¼–⅓ cup (50–100 ml) finely chopped parsley
¼ lb. (125 g) brisling anchovies
4 raw egg yolks

Peel and finely chop the onions. Dice the beets. Strain the capers.

Cut the anchovies into fine pieces. Put the anchovies on individual salad plates forming a ring towards the inner part of the plate, yet leaving the center free. Working outward, put the rest of the ingredients, separately, in decorative rings surrounding the anchovies. Finally place an egg yolk in the center of the plate to represent the "sun".

Serve with crisp bread and butter.

Gravlax
Gravad lax

Gravlax can be made from fresh or frozen salmon. The best result are attained from a center cut of a salmon weighing 5–7 pounds. The salmon should be frozen several days before curing. Curing gravlax is not difficult, but it takes a few days before the fish is ready to serve. The cured salmon can be frozen.

4–6 PORTIONS

2 lbs. (1 kg) salmon, preferably a center cut
2–3 tablespoons white peppercorns
¼ cup (50 ml) salt
¼ cup (50 ml) sugar
2 bouquets of dill
GRAVLAX SAUCE:
2–3 tablespoons prepared mustard
1 tablespoon sugar
½–1 tablespoon vinegar
¼ teaspoon salt
⅛ teaspoon white pepper
⅔ cup (150 ml) vegetable oil
2–3 tablespoons finely chopped dill

If the salmon is frozen, let it partially thaw and then fillet it in two, removing all the bones but leaving the skin attached. Dry the fillets with paper towels. Coarsely grind the peppercorns and mix together with the salt and sugar. Sprinkle some of this salt mixture evenly in a shallow baking dish together with some of the chopped dill. Place one of the fillets in the baking dish, meat side up, and sprinkle with half of the remaining salt and sugar mixture as well as a generous amount of dill. Place the other fillet, meat

Gravlax

side down, on top of the first. Finally, sprinkle with the rest of the sugar-salt mixture and the dill. Cover the baking dish and let stand in a cool place for 48 hours. Turn the salmon fillets over a couple of times during the curing process.

GRAVLAX SAUCE: Mix together the mustard, sugar, vinegar, and spices. With an electric beater or food processor, add oil to the mustard mixture in a very slow steady stream, beating constantly.

Flavor with fresh dill.

Raw Pickled Baltic Herring
Klargravad strömming

Serve these herring fillets whole as an appetizer or light meal together with gravlax sauce, see page 52, and boiled potatoes. Freeze the fish before pickling.

4 PORTIONS

2 lbs. (1 kg) small Baltic herring or 1 lb. (500 g) fillets
3 tablespoons salt per quart water
3 tablespoons chopped dill
MARINADE:
¼–⅓ cup (75–100 ml) vinegar
2 tablespoons salt
2 tablespoons sugar
2 teaspoons ground white peppercorns
⅓ cup (100 ml) oil

Clean and fillet the fish. Place fish in salted water for 2–3 hours. Remove the skin and place the fillets in a jar or glass bowl, alternating the fish with the dill.

Mix together the ingredients for the marinade and pour over the fish. Refrigerate 1–2 days.

Smoked Fish in Mustard Marinade
Senapsmarinerad rökt fisk

Serve this together with boiled potatoes and a green salad.

4 PORTIONS

1 lb. (500–600 g) smoked fish, such as smoked Baltic herring (buckling), mackerel, or whitefish

MARINADE:

1½ tablespoons vinegar

⅛ teaspoon salt

½ pinch pepper

2 tablespoons prepared mustard

4 tablespoons oil

2 tablespoons finely chopped chives

GARNISH:

½ cup (100 ml) pickled beets, finely diced

½ cup (100 ml) finely chopped fresh cucumber or sour pickles

dill (optional)

Clean and fillet the fish.

Place the fillets in a shallow bowl.

Mix together the ingredients for the marinade and pour over the fish. Marinate in the refrigerator for several hours.

Place the beets and cucumber or pickles in decorative rows on top of the fish. Garnish with dill, if desired.

Fish in Aspic
Fiskaladåb

4 PORTIONS

2–2½ lbs. (1–1¼ kg) fresh fish, such as eel or small Baltic herring

1 qt. (1 liter) water

3 teaspoons salt

5 white peppercorns

2 whole allspice berries

½–1 onion

1 small carrot, finely diced

1–2 sprigs of fresh dill

1 tablespoon vinegar essence (optional)

GELATIN:

1 sheet gelatin per ½ cup (100 ml) strained fish bouillon (use 1 envelope or 1 tablespoon gelatin per 1 cup (200 ml) of liquid)

1 egg white

Clean and scale the fish in the regular way. Slice into 2″ (5 cm) wide pieces. The small Baltic herring can be rolled together, skin side outwards. Fasten with toothpicks.

Bring the salted water and the other ingredients to a boil. Pour this hot solution over the pieces of fish. Simmer 6–10 minutes, 15–20 minutes for eel.

Let the fish cool in its own bouillon. Remove bones and skin. Place the fish in a bowl or serving dish and garnish with shrimp, dill or parsley.

Place the gelatin in cold water.

Strain the fish bouillon. Measure and heat in a saucepan. Twist or squeeze the sheet of gelatin to remove excess moisture. Add the gelatin and a slightly beaten egg white to the saucepan. Boil, stirring constantly. Cover and let the saucepan stand for 10 minutes. Strain the bouillon and allow to cool. Do not let it become firm. Pour over the fish. Refrigerate 3–5 hours. Turn the dish upside down carefully onto a serving plate and garnish with lettuce, parsley, etc.

Serve together with boiled potatoes, mayonnaise or piquante sauce, and a green salad.

Poached Fish
Inkokt fisk

Only fish such as salmon, Baltic herring, and mackerel, which are rich in oil are usually poached. The fish may be poached whole or in sections. It is not necessary to use vinegar essence, but it does reduce some of the oily taste as well as improves the consistency of the fish.

4 PORTIONS

2–2½ lbs. (1–1¼ kg) fish
1 qt. (1 liter) water
3 teaspoons salt
5 white peppercorns
2 whole allspice berries
½–1 onion or 1 piece of leek
1 small carrot (optional)
1–2 sprigs of dill
1 tablespoon vinegar essence, 12% (optional)

Clean and scale the fish. If desired, slice into 1–2" (3–4 cm) thick pieces.

Bring the water and other ingredients to a boil in a saucepan and let the solution boil for 5–10 minutes. Put the fish into the boiling solution, ensuring that the fish is completely covered by liquid. Sections of fish turn out better if the hot solution is poured over them instead.

Cover and simmer. The amount of time it takes to poach the fish depends on the size and thickness of the fish. Poach an entire fish 20–30 minutes and fish sections 6–10 minutes.

The fish may be served either hot or cold, but is most often served cold. Cool the fish as soon as possible. Place the saucepan in cold water, changing the water often.

Serve together with boiled potatoes, piquante sauce or horseradish cream.

Poached Salmon
Inkokt lax

Eliminate the vinegar essence, which bleaches the salmon, as well as the allspice. If you wish, remove the skin before serving. Pour some of the strained bouillon over the salmon or cover with a thin layer of mayonnaise.

Piquante Sauce
Skarpsås

4 PORTIONS

1 hard- boiled egg
1 raw egg yolk
1 tablespoon mustard
½ pinch white pepper
1 tablespoon vinegar
⅓–½ cup (100–150 ml) whipping cream or sour cream

Peel the hard-boiled egg and remove the yolk. Put the raw and cooked yolks together in a bowl, as well as the spices, and mix until smooth. Beat the cream, but not too stiff.

The sour cream should not be beaten. Blend the whipped cream or sour cream with the egg and spice mixture. Chop the boiled egg white and add to the sauce.

Serve this as a complement to poached fish, fried fish, smoked fish, matjes herring, and different salads.

Crayfish Herring

Crayfish Herring
Kräftströmming

This dish is quick and easy to make and can be made with either fresh or frozen fish. One can vary the flavor using spices and herbs. Serve either warm or cold.

4 PORTIONS

1 lb. (500 g) small Baltic herring fillets
1½ tablespoons salt
1 tablespoon butter or margarine
5–6 tomatoes or 1 can crushed tomatoes (approximately 16 oz./400 g)
4–5 heads of dill

Rinse the fish. Partially thaw the frozen fillets or block of fish and slice into ½″ (1 cm) thick pieces.

Salt the fish. Roll together the fillets, meat side out, and place close together in a low, wide saucepan. Add the sliced tomatoes and dill or pour the canned tomatoes over the fish. Add 1–2 tablespoons of water if necessary. Cover and simmer over low heat, 5–10 minutes depending on the thickness of the fish.

Serve with boiled tomatoes or rice and a green salad.

Fried Baltic Herring Fillets
Stekta strömmingsflundror

These filled fillets are usually served together with mashed potatoes and lingonberries.

4 PORTIONS

2 lbs. (1 kg) small Baltic herring or 1 lb. (600 g) small
   Baltic herring fillets
salt
SUGGESTED FILLINGS:
¼–⅓ cup (75–100 ml) finely chopped dill, parsley,
   and/or chives
butter or margarine
or
¼ cup (50 ml) caviar (for example, smoked cod roe)
2 tablespoons finely chopped leek
or
10–12 brisling anchovy fillets
¼ cup (50 ml) finely chopped parsley
COATING:
⅓ cup (75 ml) graham or rye flour
   or ¼ cup (50 ml) dried bread crumbs
1 tablespoon flour
FRYING:
3 tablespoons butter or margarine

Clean and fillet the fish. Partially thaw the frozen fish. Salt if desired on the meaty side.

Prepare one of the fillings: Mix the green herbs together with some butter or margarine or butter the fish with caviar and then sprinkle the chopped leek over the fillets. One can also mix together the caviar and leeks to form a smooth paste and then spread over the fillets. For the third filling, cut or slice the anchovies into smaller pieces.

Spread the flour or bread crumbs on waxed paper. Place half the fillets, skin side down, onto the waxed paper. Put a little of the filling on each of the fillets and sandwich together with the remaining fillets. Roll the herring in the flour or bread crumbs so that they are thoroughly coated on both sides.

Fry in frying pan: Brown the butter. Put the fish, a few at a time, into the frying pan and lower the heat.

Fry each side for 2–3 minutes over medium heat or until the fillets are golden brown in color and the fish is no longer transparent.

Baltic Herring in Vinegar
Ättikströmming

You'll find this on a smorgasbord or served cold for lunch together with freshly boiled potatoes and a green salad.

4 PORTIONS

1 recipe of Fried Baltic Herring filled with green herbs
PICKLING SOLUTION:
1 cup (250 ml) water
⅓ cup (75 ml) vinegar essence (12 %)
¼ cup (50 ml) sugar
5 coarsely ground allspice berries
1–2 bay leaves
GARNISH:
1–2 red onions
sprigs of dill

In a saucepan, blend together the ingredients for the pickling solution and bring to a boil. Cool.

Place the fried fish fillets in a bowl or dish. Warm fish will absorb more flavor from the pickling solution. Pour the solution over the fish. Place sliced onions and dill on top and refrigerate.

Serve after 2–3 hours, but preferably the next day.

Chimney Sweepers
Sotare

Quite simply, Chimney Sweepers are small Baltic Herring that are either barbequed or broiled until their skin is black as coal. The skin is removed after serving to reveal a moist and juicy inside that has a fantastic aroma.

4 PORTIONS

2 lbs. (1 kg) small Baltic herring, small perch,
*   or a special type of whitefish (bleak)*
salt
oil
SALT WATER:
1 qt. (1 liter) warm water
3 tablespoons salt
GREEN HERB SAUCE:
⅔ cup (150 ml) sour cream
¼–⅓ cup (50–100 ml) finely chopped chives
¼ teaspoon salt
⅛ teaspoon pepper

Clean the fish, but leave the backbone. Rinse and let drain. Rub with salt.

Brush fish with oil and place close together on a grill.

Barbeque or broil over medium or high heat so that the herring becomes blackened on both sides. Dip the barbequed or broiled fish in salt water for a second.

Blend together the ingredients for green herb sauce.

Serve the fish immediately together with potatoes and sauce.

Fried Baltic Herring in Onion and Cream Sauce
Stekt salt sill med lök och gräddsky

4 PORTIONS

4–6 salted Baltic herring fillets (1 lb./420 g)
2 white onions
COATING:
⅓ cup (100 ml) rye flour or bread crumbs and white
*   flour*
FRYING:
2 tablespoons butter or margarine
¾ cup (200 ml) whipping cream

Soak the fish in water for 10–12 hours or follow package instructions.

Drain well. Roll in the coating.

Peel and slice the onions and brown in half the butter. Place on a platter and keep warm.

Fry the fish in the remaining fat until golden brown. Place on platter next to the onions.

Add cream to the juice in the frying pan and stir well. Serve the sauce separately or pour over the fish. Serve freshly fried together with boiled potatoes.

Oven-Baked Salmon Fillets
Ugnsstekta laxfiléer

4 PORTIONS

2 lbs. (1 kg) fresh or frozen salmon
salt, pepper
1 large bouquet of dill
COATING:
2 tablespoons bread crumbs
2 tablespoons all-purpose flour
salt, pepper
FRYING:
2 tablespoons butter or margarine
1½ cups (300 ml) fish bouillon
SAUCE:
¾ cup (200 ml) fish bouillon
2 tablespons butter
1½ tablespoons all-purpose flour
1 egg yolk
⅓ cup (100 ml) whipping cream
(salt, pepper, lemon)

Partially thaw the frozen salmon and fillet.

Begin by scaling the fish. Fillet as usual, leaving the skin on the fish. Rub the fillets with salt and pepper.

Using the fish bones, make bouillon with water, salt, pepper, 1–2 dill branches, and, if necessary, one fish bouillon cube.

Clean the dill by removing the thickest branches. Chop the rest of the dill and add to the bouillon.

Brown the butter in a small roasting pan or deep baking dish. Place the largest sprigs of dill in the dish or pan.

Brush or dip the skin of the fish in the beaten egg yolk. Roll the fish in the bread crumb mixture to coat.

Place half the salmon fillets in the baking dish, meat side up, and sprinkle heavily with the chopped dill. Sandwich together the other salmon fillet on top of the first.

Place the salmon in the center of the oven and bake at 435°F (225°C) for about 15 minutes.

Baste with butter occasionally. Reduce the temperature to 350°F (175°C) and bake another 15 minutes. Place the fish on a warm serving platter and keep warm while preparing the sauce.

Add fish bouillon to the baking dish and stir, Strain bouillon and measure it.

Melt the butter for the sauce in a saucepan. Add flour and stir. Dilute with the fish bouillon, adding a little at a time. Boil 5 minutes.

Remove the saucepan from the burner. Beat the egg yolks and cream together and beat into sauce. Do not let the sauce boil! Flavor as desired with salt, pepper, and a little fresh lemon juice.

Serve at once.

Plaice Au Gratin with Mushrooms
Rödspättagratäng med champinjoner

4 PORTIONS

1 lb. (500–600 g) fillets of plaice
½–1 teaspoon salt
small can of mushroom purée (180 g)
3–4 oz. (100 g) jar of black caviar
¾ cup (200 ml) whipping cream
1 tablespoon all-purpose flour

Grease a deep baking dish.

Rinse the fresh fillets or partially thaw the frozen fillets so they can be separated from each other. Arrange in a baking dish. Season with salt. Spread the mushroom purée over the fish with a spatula and dot the fish with small teaspoonsful of caviar.

Add the flour to the cream. Beat until thick and spread over the fish. Bake in the oven 15–25 minutes until golden brown, the length of baking time depending on how frozen the fish was when placed in the oven.

Serve immediately together with rice or riced potatoes, baby peas, and a tossed salad.

Baltic Herring Casserole
Strömmingslåda

4 PORTIONS

2 lbs. (1 kg) Baltic herring or 1 lb. (500–600 g) Baltic
herring fillets (stromming)

SUGGESTED FILLINGS:

2 tablespoons caviar (for example, smoked cod roe)
3 tablespoons finely chopped dill
8 chopped brisling anchovy fillets
2 tablespoons finely chopped onion
2–3 tablespoons grated horseradish
2 tablespoons finely chopped parsley
1 tablespoon salt

FOR BAKING:

2 tablespoons butter or margarine
2 tablespoons dried bread crumbs
¼–⅓ cup (50–100 ml) of cream or milk
1 tablespoon tomato paste

Clean the herring, removing the heads and back-
bones. Rinse and pat dry.

Rub with salt. Put on a chopping board, skin side
down, and put a spoonful of filling on each fillet.

Roll or sandwich together the herring and place in
a greased baking dish. Sprinkle with bread crumbs
and dot with butter.

Bake in the oven at 435°F (225°C) for 20 minutes.
Toward the end of baking, baste with a mixture of
cream or milk mixed with a little tomato paste for a
moister casserole.

Serve as part of a smorgasbord or together with a
tossed salad for lunch.

Jansson's Temptation
Janssons frestelse

This is one of the most well-known dishes in Sweden
and is served on a smorgasbord, for lunch, or as a late
night supper. It can be prepared ahead of time and then
reheated later using a little extra cream or milk.

4 PORTIONS

8–10 potatoes
2 onions
20 brisling anchovy fillets
1¼ cups (300 ml) whipping cream
1 tablespoon dried bread crumbs
1 tablespoon butter or margarine

Peel the potatoes and onions. Coarsely shred the potatoes. Slice or chop the onion and sauté it in a little
butter or margarine 5 minutes.

Alternate layers of potatoes, onion, and anchovies
in a lightly greased baking dish, the top and bottom
layers consisting of potatoes.

Pour half the cream and 2–3 tablespoons anchovy
juice over the casserole. Dot with butter and sprinkle
with bread crumbs.

Bake in the oven at 435°F (225°C) for 45 minutes.
Baste the outer edges of the casserole with the remaining cream towards the end of the 45 minutes.

Serve together with bread, butter, cheese, and a
tossed salad.

Jansson's Temptation

Oven-Baked Eel
Ugnsstekt ål

Serve the eel warm with boiled potatoes, lemon slices, piquante sauce, and a green salad.

4–5 PORTIONS

1½–2 lbs. (¾–1 kg) fresh eel
2 teaspoons salt
fresh lemon juice (optional)
COATING:
1 egg
3 tablespoons bread crumbs
½ teaspoon salt
⅛ teaspoon pepper

Clean and skin the eel. Cut a deep slit through the tough skin just behind the head. Hold the head in place with paper, and pull the skin off using pliers or a tong. The easiest way of doing this is to nail the head of the eel to a thick board.

Notch the back of the eel. Sprinkle with salt and drip lemon juice over the back of the eel.

Grease a round baking dish and place the eel in a ring in the pan. Brush with the beaten egg and sprinkle bread crumbs over the eel. Place in the center of the oven at 480°F (250°C). Reduce temperature to 435°F (225°C) and bake for 30 minutes. Baste the eel with the fat in the baking dish. Sprinkle with freshly chopped dill.

Salmon Pudding
Laxpudding

4 PORTIONS

1 lb. (400 g) salted salmon or rainbow trout, or lightly salt-cured salmon
8–10 peeled potatoes
1 onion (optional)
EGG MIXTURE:
4 eggs
1⅔ cups (400 ml) milk
⅛ teaspoon white pepper
2 tablespoons finely chopped dill
FOR BAKING:
1 tablespoon butter or margarine

Soak the salted salmon or trout in water for about 12 hours, depending on its salt content. The salt-cured salmon does not require soaking.

Cut the fish into very thin slices or strips. Slice the potatoes and optional onion.

Grease a baking dish. Put salmon, onions, and potatoes in alternating layers into the baking dish, finishing with a layer of potatoes.

Beat together the egg, milk, and pepper. Pour this mixture into the baking dish. Bake at 435°F (225°C) until the pudding has set, about 45–60 minutes.

Sprinkle with fresh dill.

Serve with melted butter and a green salad.

Herring Pudding
Sillpudding

Follow the same recipe as above only substituting ½ lb. salt herring fillets for the salmon. Soak the fillets 10–12 hours prior to preparation or follow the package directions.

Fish Paté
Fiskpaté

6–8 PORTIONS

1 lb. (400 g) fillet of salmon
½ lb. (250 g) frozen broccoli
FISH MIXTURE:
1 lb. (400 g) fish fillets of haddock or pike
1 egg white
1 teaspoon salt
1¼ cup (300 ml) whipping cream
⅛ teaspoon pepper
½ teaspoon tarragon
SAUCE:
¼ cup (50 ml) chopped dill
¼ cup (50 ml) chopped parsley
¾ cup (200 ml) light crème fraiche or sour cream light
⅓ cup (100 ml) mayonnaise

Cut the skinless and boneless salmon into ¾" (1½ cm) cubes. Break the broccoli into smaller pieces. Remove the thickest part of the stalk. Boil the broccoli according to package directions and drain well.

Chop the salmon in a food processor. Add salt, egg white, and cream, a little at a time. Season to taste.

Fold the salmon and broccoli into the fish mixture. Pour into a 1½ qt. oblong baking dish that has been brushed with cooking oil.

Shake the baking dish so that the mixture becomes compact. Smooth the surface. Cover with aluminum foil and bake in the center of the oven for one hour at 350°F (175°C).

Allow to cool and remove carefully from baking dish. Slice.

Mix together ingredients for the sauce.

Serve with bread and salad.

Fish Tureen
Fiskterrin

4 PORTIONS

1 lb. (400 g) fish fillets (pike-perch, haddock, or cod)
¼ cup (50 ml) chopped parsley
2 eggs
¾ cup (200 ml) crème fraiche or whipping cream
¼ cup (50 ml) liquid from mussels and crabs
⅛ teaspoon nutmeg
1½ teaspoon salt
⅛ teaspoon white pepper
1 can crabmeat (approximately 6 oz./175 g)
1 can mussels or clams in water (approximately 8 oz./225 g)

Finely chop the fillets of fish in a food processor. Add parsley, eggs, crème fraiche, liquids, spices, and crab meat. Blend well using the blade of the processor. Carefully fold in the mussels.

Pour the mixture into a 1½ qt. greased baking dish. Cover and bake one hour at 350°F (175°C).

This tureen is delicious served warm together with a shrimp, wine, or lemon sauce or served cold together with sour cream that is flavored with green herbs.

IN THE MICROWAVE: Pour the mixture into a suitable dish and cover. Heat on high for 10–12 minutes.

Lutfisk

Oven-Poached Lutfish
Kokt lutfisk i ugn

<u>4 PORTIONS</u>

3–4 lbs. (1½–2 kg) frozen lutfish
1 tablespoons salt
1–2 tablespoons of butter or margarine, for greasing the pan

Thaw the frozen fish completely according to package instructions. Grease a deep baking dish with butter or margarine. Place the fish, skin side down, in the dish or skin the fish before boiling, if prefered. If the skin is removed, the fish will not curl up and be easier to eat. Sprinkle the fish with salt.

Cover with aluminum foil and let the lutfish poach in the oven in its own juice at 435°F (225°C) for 40–55 minutes. Remove from oven and pour off the excess liquid.

Dine on warm lutfish together with boiled potatoes, sauce or melted butter, mustard, and peas.

Boiled Lutfish
Kokt lutfisk i gryta

Prepare the fish as above. Place in a boiling or roasting bag. Boil the fish in a large saucepan or kettle or follow the package directions. One can also place the fish, skin side down in a stainless steel kettle. Salt and add ½ cup water per 2 lbs. lutfish. Cover and simmer slowly for 20 minutes. Remove the fish with a large perforated ladle. Serve as above.

Lutfish Sauce
Vit grundsås

Lutfish is usually served with a basic white sauce and green peas. In Skåne they often serve lutfish together with a mustard sauce.

4 PORTIONS

2 tablespoons butter or margarine
3 tablespoons flour
1½–2 cups (450–500 ml) milk
⅛ teaspoon salt
½ pinch white pepper

Melt the butter in a saucepan over low heat. Remove from the burner. Stir in flour. Add all the milk at once. Put the saucepan back on the burner and bring sauce to a boil while stirring. Let boil 3–5 minutes.

Mustard Sauce from Skåne

Crush 1–2½ tablespoons brown mustard seed in a mortel. Add very little water, but enough so that its consistency is thick like porridge. Flavor a basic white sauce with this mixture and add just a pinch of sugar.

Fish in a Jacket
Fisk i kapprock

The flavor of the fish is enhanced when it is baked in a jacket of greased paper or aluminum foil. Prepare the dish in individual portions and serve after guests have been seated. Everyone should have his own package to open.

4 PORTIONS

1 lb. (500 g) fish fillets of trout, plaice, whiting, etc.
*   or 4 well-drained salted Baltic herring fillets*
1 teaspoon salt
⅛ teaspoon pepper
2 tablespoons butter or margarine
2 tablespoons finely-chopped dill or chopped onion
*   and/or chives*

Rub the fillets with salt and pepper. Cut out large circles of greased paper or aluminum foil. Grease the center of the paper or foil with a little margarine.

Place a fish fillet on each piece of paper or foil and cover with dill and onions. Place a dab of butter on each fillet. Fold the package together tightly.

Fry the package in a warm frying pan on both sides until the paper turns brown, about 10 minutes, or bake in the oven at 480°F (250°C) for about 10 minutes. If using aluminum foil, the fish must be baked in the oven.

Place the packages on a platter. Do not open until they have been placed on the plates.

Serve with boiled potatoes and a salad of Chinese cabbage and carrots.

Vegetables

The Swedish climate, with its light summer nights, produces vegetables that have an especially fine aroma. Here are recipes for everything from ribboned vegetable paté to "long kale" from Halland, its name a derivation from how it ,traditionally, was prepared. The housewives from Halland mixed their kale together with ham broth and cream, adding a little at a time, letting it simmer over low heat until the consistency was very smooth.

You can also find recipes for local potato dishes and musty mushroom dishes capturing the scent of autumn. In Sweden picking mushrooms is not a lost art, and you can find mushroom enthusiasts scampering about in the Swedish forests from early to late autumn in search of the many different types excellent edible mushrooms that are bountiful there.

Summer Casserole
Sommargryta

4 PORTIONS

1 small head of cauliflower
1 bunch of tender carrots (about ½ lb.)
6–8 small fresh potatoes
1 cup (200–300 ml) vegetable bouillon
½ lb. (150 g) sugar peas
4–5 green onions or 1 tender leek
parsley

Clean the cauliflower and divide into bouquets. Scrape and slice the carrots. Brush and scrape the potatoes. Pour a little of the bouillon over the vegetables in a saucepan. Cover and boil about 15 minutes until vegetables are barely tender. Clean the sugar peas and onion or leek. Divide the onions into 2–3 pieces if necessary and slice the leek into 2" (5 cm) slices. Add the peas and onions to the saucepan. Boil 5–10 minutes more. Sprinkle with finely chopped parsley.

Serve warm with bread. It is a good complement to lightly smoked ham, smoked pork, or smoked fish.

Vegetables in White Sauce
Stuvade grönsaker

Most vegetables can be creamed alone or together in different combinations. Always start by first preparing the vegetable needing the longest cooking time.

4 PORTIONS

2½–3 cups (500–700 g) vegetables
1 teaspoon salt per quart water
WHITE SAUCE:
2 tablespoons butter or margarine
3 tablespoons all-purpose flour
1½–1¾ cup (300–400 ml) vegetable bouillon and milk
½ teaspoon salt
⅛ teaspoon pepper
parsley (optional)

Clean and cut the vegetables into smaller pieces.

Boil them in lightly salted water until barely soft. Pour off the broth and set aside.

Make the white sauce: Melt the butter or margarine in a saucepan; stir in the flour and dilute with the vegetable bouillon and milk. Allow to simmer several minutes, stirring often. Season to taste.

Summer Casserole

Ribboned Vegetable Paté
Randig grönsakspaté

6 PORTIONS

SPINACH PURÉE:

2 lbs. (1 kg) pounds fresh spinach or 3/4 lb. (400 g)
    frozen chopped spinach
2 teaspoons potato flour
3 tablespoons crème fraiche or whipping cream
1 egg
¼ teaspoon salt
⅛ teaspoon ground nutmeg

CARROT PURÉE:

3–4 medium-sized carrots (¾ lb.)
1 teaspoon potato flour
3 tablespoons crème fraiche or whipping cream
1 egg
¼ teaspoon salt
⅛ teaspoon white pepper

PARSNIP PURÉE:

1–2 parsnips (¾ lb.)
1 teaspoon flour
3 tablespoons crème fraiche or whipping cream
1 egg
¼ teaspoon salt
⅛ teaspoon white pepper

Clean the fresh spinach and parboil in boiling water. Drain well. Mix or finely chop in a food processor. Thaw the frozen spinach and drain well. Try to squeeze out as much liquid as possible from the spinach (twist in a towel or squeeze in paper towels). This will keep the the paté from being runny.

Peel carrots and parsnips. Cover with water and and boil separately on top of the stove or in a microwave oven until soft.

Drain well. Twist in a towel to remove excess moisture. Purée carrots and parsnips separately in a food processor or mixer. Blend each purée together with potato flour, crème fraiche, egg, and spices. Grease a bread pan or deep baking dish . Pour the purées into the form in layers , starting with the spinach, followed by the carrots, and then finally the parsnips. Cover.

Bake on a rack in the lower part of the oven for 50–60 minutes at 350°F (175°C). Allow to cool and remove from baking form. Serve in slices with a green herb sour cream sauce.

Vegetables au Gratin
Gratinerade grönsaker med ostsås

4 PORTIONS

3¼ cups (750 g) boiled vegetables

CHEESE SAUCE:

2 tablespoons butter or margarine
3 tablespoons all-purpose flour
1⅔ cups (400 ml) milk
½ cup (100–150 ml) cheese (Herrgård or Svecia,
    for example)
1 egg yolk (optional)
½–1 teaspoon salt
⅛ teaspoon pepper
⅛ teaspoon grated nutmeg

TOPPING:

½ cup (100 ml) grated cheese

Melt the butter or margarine in a saucepan over low heat. Remove from heat. Stir in the flour and add all the milk at once. Place the saucepan back on the burner and boil 3–5 minutes, stirring constantly. Remove from heat. Add the grated cheese and allow it to melt.

Mix in a little milk with the egg yolk. Beat into the sauce. Let sauce simmer a couple of minutes while stirring. Do not let the sauce the boil, as it will curdle and the cheese will become tough and stringy.

Flavor with salt, pepper, and nutmeg. Pour sauce over the vegetables. Sprinkle with grated cheese and bake at 480°F (250°C), the best temperature for a topping that will turn out nice and even.

Ribboned Vegetable Paté

Green Pie
Grön paj

6 PORTIONS

PIE DOUGH:
⅔ cup (150 g) butter or margarine
1⅓ cups (300 ml) all-purpose flour
3 tablespoons water
FILLING:
1 cup (250 g) broccoli
2 cups (500 g) spinach
1 large leek
1 bouquet of parsley
water
1 teaspoon salt per quart (liter) water
2 teaspoons butter or margarine
1–2 cloves of garlic
3 eggs
1⅔ cups (400 ml) milk and cream
2 cups (400–500 ml) grated aged cheese
pepper
salt (optional)

Blend together ingredients for the pie dough.

Clean and rinse the broccoli. Boil in lightly-salted water until almost tender. Drain well. Slice into pieces. Clean the spinach and parboil several minutes in lightly salted water. Drain well.

Rinse the leek and slice. Sauté lightly in butter. Add the spinach and pressed cloves of garlic.

Roll out the pie dough. Line the bottom and sides of a small rectangular baking pan (8″×10″ or 20×30 cm) with the dough. Fold a strip of aluminum foil around the top of the form, covering the edges of the pie. Bake the pie shell for about 10 minutes at 400°F (200°C).

Remove the foil. Spread a layer of cheese on the bottom of the pie shell, followed by a layer of broccoli, the sautéed mixture, and finally chopped parsley.

Beat the eggs together with the milk. Add salt and pepper to taste. Sprinkle the remaining cheese over the vegetables. Pour egg mixture over the pie.

Bake the pie in the lower part of the oven for about 30 minutes.

Serve slightly cooled.

Vegetable Soufflé
Grönsakssufflé

4 SERVINGS

1 lb. (500 g) boiled vegetables, either one sort or
    a combination of different vegetables
¼ cup (50 g) butter or margarine
4 tablespoons all-purpose flour
1⅓ cups (300 ml) milk
1 tablespoon corn starch
4 egg yolks
salt, pepper
1⅓ cups (300 ml) grated cheese (optional)
4 egg whites

Drain the vegetables well. Slice into smaller pieces.

Melt the butter a saucepan and let sizzle a few minutes. Sprinkle with flour and stir. Dilute with milk, adding a little at a time, stirring often until sauce is smooth. Remove from heat and stir vigorously so that the sauce cools somewhat. Mix together the egg yolks and cornstarch and add to the sauce. Flavor with salt, pepper, and cheese, if desired. Add the vegetables.

Beat egg whites until stiff. Carefully, fold into the vegetable mixture. Pour into a well-greased 2½ qt. soufflé form, filling only ⅔ full.

Bake the soufflé in the lower part of the oven for about 45 minutes at 350°F (175°C). Serve immediately with melted or whipped butter.

Green Timbales
Gröna timbaler

4 PORTIONS

1 cup (250 g) broccoli, fresh or frozen
2 eggs
¼ cup (75 ml) whipping cream
salt, pepper
⅛ teaspoon ground nutmeg

Clean and rinse the fresh broccoli. Slice into smaller pieces. Boil until barely tender in lightly salted water. Drain well. Chop the broccoli either by hand or with a food processor or mixer.

Beat the egg and cream together and blend in with the broccoli. Flavor to taste.

Grease timbale forms or make small forms of aluminum foil and pour in the broccoli mixture. Place the forms in a shallow roasting pan filled with a little water. Cover with aluminum foil. Bake at 430°F (220°C) for about 30 minutes.

Remove the timbales from their forms while warm. Serve together with fried or roasted meat dishes.

Brown Cabbage
Brunkål

4 PORTIONS

½ head of green cabbage (about 2 lbs./1 kg)
1–2 tablespoons corn syrup
2 tablespoons Chinese soy sauce
1 cup (200–300 ml) bouillon
salt, pepper
butter or margarine (optional)

Rinse the cabbage and slice into small cubes. Remove the core. Boil in a large saucepot filled with lightly-salted water for about 10 minutes. Let drain completely. Place the drained cabbage in a shallow roasting pan.

Drizzle the syrup over the cabbage and add soy sauce. Stir well. Add the bouillon. If desired, cover with aluminum foil. Bake at 400°F (200°C) for about 1 hour in the center of the oven or until the cabbage feels very soft. Season with salt and pepper.

Serve the cabbage together with fried pork dishes, Christmas ham, smoked pork chops, or sausages.

Red Cabbage
Rödkål

This is one of the main staples of the Swedish smorgasbord.

4–8 PORTIONS

2 lbs. (1 kg) red cabbage
2 tablespoons butter, margarine, or oil
⅛–¼ cup (25–50 ml) corn syrup
2 apples
3 tablespoons vinegar
½ tablespoon salt
⅛ teaspoon pepper
¼ cup (50 ml) black currant fruit syrup or red wine (optional)

Clean and finely shred the cabbage.

Melt butter in a saucepot. Add the cabbage and drizzle with syrup. Let sizzle a few minutes, while stirring.

Peel and slice the apples in wedges. Add to the cabbage together with the vinegar. Boil until the cabbage is soft, about ½–1 hour. Stir occasionally. Flavor with salt, pepper, and the optional fruit syrup or wine.

Long Kale
Långkål

Serve the kale together with boiled ham and fried dishes of pork, cabbage, or duck.

4 PORTIONS

½–1 bunch (1 lb./500 g) kale or 1 package kale, frozen chopped
water or ham broth
1 teaspoon salt per quart water/ham broth
1 tablespoon butter of margarine
⅓ cup (50–100 ml) whipping cream or crème fraiche
salt (optional)
1–2 pinches of pepper

Remove the outer leaves from the kale. Rinse well. Place kale in saucepot and cover with lightly-salted water or the ham broth from a new boiled ham. Boil until tender. Remove the kale; drain well and chop coarsely.

Thaw the frozen kale and drain.

Let the kale sizzle in butter until shiny, stirring often. Dilute with cream or crème fraiche, adding a little at time. Season with pepper and, if necessary, a little salt.

Boiled Brown Beans
Kokta bruna bönor

Brown beans are served together with fried pork, meat-balls, or sausage.

4 PORTIONS

1⅔ cups (400 ml) brown beans
1 qt. (1 liter) water
1 teaspoon salt
2 teaspoons vinegar essence
2–3 tablespoons corn syrup or 1 tablespoon of sugar
salt (optional)
1 tablespoon flour (optional)
1 tablespoon potato flour (optional)

Soak the beans 8–10 hours in salted water. Drain. Cover and boil in salted water for 1½–2 hours or until they are soft. Beans that have not been pre-soaked need to boil at least 2 hours in 1½ qts. water. The boiling time will vary depending on the quality and age of the beans. Newly harvested beans cook faster than older beans.

Flavor the beans with vinegar essence, syrup or sugar, and perhaps a little salt.

If necessary, thicken the beans with flour mixed with a little water. Bring to a boil.

Boiled Potatoes
Kokt potatis

4 PORTIONS

8–10 potatoes
water
1 teaspoon salt per quart (liter) water
green herbs, such as dill or parsley

UNPEELED POTATOES: Brush the potatoes well. Place in a saucepan and add enough water to cover the potatoes. The water does not need to be salted. The salt will not soak through the peels. Boil 20 minutes.

PEELED POTATOES: Rinse the potatoes, peel them, and place in a saucepan. Add water and salt. Boil 20 minutes.

FRESH POTATOES: Brush or scrape the potatoes. Place in boiling, salted water. Add a few sprigs of dill. Bring to a quick boil and let boil, covered, 15–20 minutes until soft.

BOILED RICE POTATOES: Peel and cook the potatoes. Pour off the water and let the potatoes steam in the saucepan. Press the potatoes through a ricer directly into a serving dish.

Serve the potatoes at once. Sprinkle finely-cut green herbs just prior to serving.

Potatoes au Gratin
Potatisgratäng med ostsås

4 PORTIONS

8–10 potatoes
2 onions
CHEESE SAUCE:
1 tablespoon butter or margarine
3 tablespoons flour
2 cups (500 ml) milk
salt, pepper
½ teaspoon caraway
1 cup (200 ml) grated cheese

Peel and slice the potatoes and onion. Place slices in cold water.

Melt butter or margarine together with the flour in a saucepan and let boil 3 minutes stirring often. Flavor with salt, pepper, and caraway. Add the cheese.

Let the potatoes and onion drain on a paper towel. Place half the mixture in a greased baking dish and pour over half the sauce. Place the rest of the potatoes and onion in the baking dish, cover with the sauce, and finally sprinkle with cheese.

Bake in the center of the oven at 400°F (200°C) for about 45 minutes.

Serve together with cold cuts or boiled vegetables.

Creamed Potatoes
Råstuvad potatis

4 PORTIONS

8–10 potatoes
½ tablespoon butter or margarine
1½ cups (300–400 ml) milk
1 teaspoon salt
¼ teaspoon pepper

Peel and dice the potatoes into 1″ (2 cm) cubes or slice them.

Melt the cooking fat in a saucepan. Add the milk. Add the potatoes and slowly simmer, stirring occasionally until the potatoes are soft. Salt and pepper and add other spices or herbs to taste.

Serve the potatoes together with fried pork, sausages, smoked fish, meat, etc.

Hasselback Potatoes
Hasselbackspotatis

4 PORTIONS

10–12 potatoes of uniform size
2 tablespoons butter or margarine
1 teaspoon salt
1 tablespoon bread crumbs (optional)
2 tablespoons dry grated cheese

Peel potatoes. Slice the potatoes into thin slices, but not all the way through. The bottom of the potatoes should be whole. If desired, slice the bottom of the potato so it is flat and easier to place in the baking dish. Place the potatoes with the sliced side upwards in a frying pan, roasting pan, or baking dish.

Brush the tops with butter and place in the center of the oven. Baste with melted butter while baking.

Bake 45 minutes at 450°F (225°C). Sprinkle with salt, optional bread crumbs, and the grated cheese before removing from oven.

Rårakor
Rårakor

4 PORTIONS

8–10 potatoes
1 teaspoon salt
FRYING:
3 tablespoons butter, margarine, or oil

Peel and grate the potatoes, preferably with a food processor. Add salt. If the batter is so stiff that it doesn't spread out in the rying pan, thin with a little water.

Brown the fat and put about ⅛–¼ cup batter into a frying pan. Fry until crisp and brown. Serve hot.

Raggmunkar
Raggmunkar

4 PORTIONS

1 cup (200 ml) flour
1 teaspoon salt
freshly ground pepper
2 cups (500 ml) milk
1 egg
8–9 potatoes
¼ cup (25 g) butter or margarine or 1 tablespoon oil

Blend together the flour, spices, and a little of the milk so that it forms a smooth batter. Add the rest of the milk and the egg.

Peel and rinse the potatoes and coarsely grate them using either a grater or a food processor. Stir the grated potatoes into the egg mixture.

Heat the fat in a frying pan. Put a little of the batter into the frying pan and spread out with a spatula. Fry until crisp and golden brown on both sides.

Swedish Root Vegetables Casserole
Svensk rotfruktsgryta

4 PORTIONS

2 onions
¼ turnip (½ lb./250 g)
2 carrots (⅓ lb./200 g)
¼ celleriac (½ lb./250 g)
1 parsnip
1 lb. (400 g) can crushed tomatoes
salt (optional)
¼ teaspoons coarsely ground black pepper
1 bay leaf
2 teaspoons dried thyme
1⅓ cups (300 ml) vegetable bouillon (optional)
parsley

Peel onions and clean the vegetables. Chop the onion and dice the vegetables. Mix together all the ingredients in a kettle. Cover and let simmer over low heat until the vegetables are soft. Dilute with the bouillon if needed. Sprinkle with chopped parsley.

Serve the casserole together with fried pork or sausages.

Potato Dumplings from Öland
Öländska kroppkakor

These are served as a main course, together with lingonberry jam and perhaps melted butter, if desired.

4 PORTIONS

8–10 raw potatoes
4 boiled potatoes
¾ cup (200 ml) flour
1 teaspoon salt
FILLING:
¾ lb. (200 g) lightly salted side of pork
1 white or red onion
½–1 teaspoon ground allspice
FOR BOILING:
2 qts. (2 liter) water
1 tablespoon salt

Peel and finely grate the raw potatoes using either a grater or a food processor. Wring out the excess moisture in the grated potatoes by wrapping them in a towel, a little at a time, and twisting hard.

Mix the raw potatoes together with the mashed boiled potatoes. Add flour and salt and roll the dough flat into a rectangular shape. Slice into 12 pieces.

Make the filling: Dice the pork. Peel and finely chop the onion. Brown the pork in a frying pan. Add onions and allow to sizzle. Add spices and stir again.

Place a tablespoon of filling in the center of each section of potato dough. Form into round dumplings, the centers of which are filled with the pork mixture. Flatten slightly. Bring the water and salt to a boil. Add the potato dumplings, a few at a time, and boil 20 minutes after they have risen to the surface of the water.

Potato Dumplings from Öland

Potato Dumplings from Piteå
Pitepalt

4 PORTIONS

10–12 raw potatoes
1½ teaspoon salt
1¼ cup (300 ml) cornmeal
½–¾ cup (100–200 ml) flour
FILLING:
½ lb. (300 g) lightly salted side of pork
FOR BOILING:
4 qts. (4 liter) water
2 tablespoons salt

Peel, rinse, and grate or mince the potatoes. Press out as much moisture as possible. Blend the potatoes together with the salt and flour until the dough is rather stiff. Roll out to a loaf and slice into 14–16 pieces.

Finely dice the pork. Brown them in a frying pan and let sizzle a little while.

Put a little of the filling in the center of each section of potato dough and shape into round dumplings, the centers of which are filled with the fried pork mixture. Flatten slightly. Bring water to a boil in a large kettle and add the potato dumplings. Let simmer 45–60 minutes.

Remove the dumplings from the kettle with a perforated ladle. Serve as a main course together with with lingonberry jam, soft whey-cheese, or melted butter and syrup.

Mashed Turnips

Mashed Turnips
Rotmos

4 PORTIONS

1–2 turnips (about 2 lbs./1 kg)
2 carrots (optional)
6 potatoes
water, salt
1–2 tablespoons butter or margarine (optional)
salt, pepper

Peel the turnips, carrots and potatoes. Slice them in cubes or pieces. Place turnips in a saucepan and cover with lightly salted water. Cook for about 30 minutes on top of the stove or use a microwave oven.

Add carrots which are optional but add color and enhance the flavor of the dish.. Boil for another 10 minutes. Add the potatoes next, and let everything boil together until the turnips are very soft.

Drain the broth and set aside. Mash the turnips and potatoes with an electric mixer or in a food processor. Dilute with vegetable broth and add a little butter or margarine for a richer taste. Season with salt and pepper.

Serve warm, together with boiled or lightly smoked meat or sausage.

Creamy Mushroom Stew
Gräddig svamppanna

4 PORTIONS

1 small onion
2–3 cups (1–1½ qts./1–1½ liter) fresh mushrooms, such
*   as funnelshaped autumn chanterelles (höstkantareller)*
*   or scaly ink caps (fjällig bläcksvamp)*
2 tablespoons butter or margarine
1⅓ cups (300 ml) cream
½ tablespoon butter or margarine
½ tablespoon flour
salt, pepper
½ teaspoon chervil
chopped parsley

Peel and finely chop the onion. Clean the mushrooms and slice into smaller pieces if necessary.

Melt the butter or margarine in a frying pan and lightly sauté the onion. Add the mushrooms and sauté them until all liquid has evaporated from the pan.

Dilute with cream and let simmer until the cream thickens, about 10 minutes. For a thicker consistency, make a paste of butter and flour and add to the stew while stirring.

Flavor with salt, pepper, and chervil. Sprinkle with parsley.

Serve the mushrooms with toast for lunch or as an evening snack or together with cold boiled ham.

Mushroom Goulash
Svampgryta

For best results, use several different sorts of mushrooms to make this goulash – for example, smörsopp (ringed boletus), karljohansvamp (cep), and taggsvamp (hedgehog mushrooms).

4 PORTIONS

1–2 onions
2 tablespoons butter or margarine
2 cups (1 qt./1 liter) mixed mushrooms
1 teaspoon paprika
1 cup (250 ml) water
½ bouillon cube
2 tablespoons flour
2 tablespoons butter or margarine
salt, pepper
⅛ teaspoon allspice
⅓ cup (100 ml) crème fraiche or whipping cream
4 tomatoes
green herbs

Peel the onion and slice into wedges. Sauté in butter or margarine without browning

Add the cleaned and sliced mushrooms and let them simmer until all liquid has evaporated.

Sprinkle with paprika and add the water and bouillon cube.

Make a paste of flour and butter. Put into the saucepan and stir until the sauce is smooth and thick.

Season with salt, pepper and allspice.

Stir in the crème fraiche and let simmer 3–4 minutes, stirring occasionally.

Dip the tomatoes into boiling water and remove the peels. Slice into wedges and add to the goulash. Sprinkle with herbs.

Serve with rice.

Pancakes, Waffles, and Egg Dishes

We talked a good deal about porridge, gruel, and other grain -based dishes in the beginning of this book. It is the custom to serve waffles on March 25th, Annunciation Day, in Sweden. All children love pancake torte with its alternating layers of jam and whipped cream. This is also a special summer treat when one has access to sun-ripened blueberries and wild strawberries.

Pancakes and Small Pancakes
Pannkakor och plättar

The small pancakes are fried on a special griddle called a plättpanna (platt pan) or in a frying pan.

ABOUT 12 PANCAKES/50 SMALL PANCAKES

3 eggs
2½ cups (600 ml) milk
1 cup (250 ml) flour
½ teaspoon salt
2–3 tablespoons butter or margarine

Beat eggs, half the milk, all the flour and salt together until well-blended and without lumps. Add the rest of milk.

Melt the butter and beat into the batter.

Heat up a pancake griddle or frying pan with sloping sides. If necessary, grease the griddle before frying the first pancake. The remaining pancakes will not require greasing.

Pour about ½ cup of pancake batter on the griddle. Lower the heat. Fry until the surface becomes dull, and the underside is golden brown.

Turn and fry the other side.

Stir the batter occasionally so the flour doesn't sink to the bottom.

Stack the pancakes, folded or rolled together, on a serving platter.

Serve together with jam, apple sauce, or fresh berries, mashed, as a dessert or after soup.

Small Carrot Pancakes
Morotsplättar

ABOUT 50 PANCAKES

4 medium carrots (almost 3/4 lb./300 g)
4 eggs
1½ cup (400 ml) milk
¾ cup (200 ml) flour
1 teaspoon salt
3 tablespoons butter or margarine

Peel and finely grate the carrots, preferably in a food processor.

Beat together the eggs and half the milk. Add flour and salt. Beat batter until smooth and without lumps. Pour in the remaining milk. Add carrots and mix.

Melt butter and pour into the batter, saving enough melted butter to grease the pancake griddle once in the beginning.

Heat up a *plättpanna* (a special pancake griddle for making several small pancakes at the same time). Grease it. Pour about 1 tablespoon of batter in each depression in the griddle. Fry until the batter sets on top side. Turn, and fry the other side.

Serve the pancakes hot for lunch or as light supper dish together with a salad of lettuce and small pieces of lemon or together with chilled sour cream flavored with finely grated leeks.

Blueberry Pancakes
Blåbärspannkaka

4–6 SERVINGS

2 eggs
1⅔ cups (400 ml) milk
⅔ cup (150 ml) flour
pinch of salt
1 tablespoon butter or margarine
1 cup fresh blueberries (250 ml) or one package
    (1 cup or 8 oz./225 g) frozen blueberries
sugar to taste
GARNISH:
powdered sugar

Beat the eggs together with half the milk. Add flour and salt and beat until batter is smooth, without any lumps. Add the remaining milk.

Pour the batter into a greased cast- iron frying pan with straight sides or into a 10″ (24 cm) round baking form.

Bake in the lower part of the oven at 435°F (225°C) for about 15 minutes.

Add the berries (Frozen berries don't need to be thawed) and bake another 15 minutes until the batter is firm and golden brown in color.

Cool several minutes before serving. Serve together with ice cream or whipped cream.

TIPS: The blueberries can be substituted with pitted cherries, fresh currants, or lingonberries.

Crêpes à la Prince Bertil
Crêpes à la prins Bertil

12–15 CRÊPES

CRÊPES:
⅓ cup (100 ml) water
⅓ cup (100 ml) flour
⅓ cup (100 ml) whipping cream
3 eggs
¼ teaspoon salt
1 tablespoon melted butter or margarine
FILLING:
3 egg yolks
⅔ cup (150 g) melted butter
3 teaspoon fresh lemon juice
1 lb. (300–500 g) shrimp, boiled and unpeeled
    (approximately)
3–4 tablespoons fresh dill, finely chopped
FOR BAKING:
grated cheese

Mix together water, flour, and cream until smooth and free of lumps. Beat in the eggs, salt, and butter.

Heat crêpes pan. Grease before frying the first crêpe. Pour in a thin layer of batter in the crêpe pan. Fry until the top is completely firm. Only one side needs to be fried.

Stack the crêpes on top of one another, separating them with thin pieces of paper. Keep warm until filled.

Prepare the filling. Peel the shrimp (and drain if necessary).

Place the egg yolks in the top of a double boiler and heat over warm water. Add the melted butter in a thin stream, beat vigorously until the sauce is thick and shiny.

Stir in the well-drained shrimp (cut the shrimp into smaller pieces if necessary) and the dill.

Place a little of the shrimp filling on each crêpe. Roll together and place seam-side- down in a greased ovenproof dish. Sprinkle with grated cheese.

Bake at 435°F (225°C) for 6–7 minutes. Serve at once.

Pancake Torte
Pannkakstårta

4 PORTIONS

3 eggs
2½ cups (600 ml) milk
½ teaspoon salt
2 teaspoons sugar
1 cup (250 ml) flour
2–3 teaspoons butter or margarine
FILLING:
1–1½ cups (200–300 ml) jam or 1½ cups (300 ml)
   lightly sweetened berry preserves
GARNISH:
3–4 tablespoons jam or jelly

Beat the eggs together with half the milk. Add salt, sugar, and all the flour. Beat or stir until batter is smooth and without lumps. Add the rest of the milk.

Melt the butter and add to the batter.

Heat a pancake griddle or frying pan 10″ (26 cm) in diameter. Grease prior to frying the first pancake. The other pancakes do not need greasing. Pour a little less than ½ cup (1 dl) of batter on the griddle for each pancake. Fry on medium heat until the surface is firmly set and is golden brown on the underside. Turn and fry on the other side until the pancake browns.

Stack the pancakes directly onto a serving plate and spread a filling of jam between the layers.

TIPS: For a really festive pancake torte, garnish with ½–¾ cup (100–200 ml) whipped cream. Frost the top just before serving. The whipped cream can also be piped decoratively on the cake. Garnish with small dollops of jam or jelly or with fresh berries.

Oven Pancake with Pork
Ugnspannkaka med fläsk

4–6 SERVINGS

¾ lb. (300 g) lightly smoked bacon or side of pork
3 eggs
3¼ cups (800 ml) milk
1¾ cups (400 ml) flour

Set oven to 435°F (225°C).

Slice the pork into small cubes. Place in a rectangular baking dish, about 12″×18″ (30×40 cm) in size. Place in oven and brown. Stir occasionally so the pork browns evenly.

Beat the eggs. Add half the milk and all the flour to eggs and beat until batter is smooth and without lumps. Stir in the remaining milk. Pour the batter into the baking pan and place it in the middle of the oven.

Bake 25–30 minutes until the pancake is completely firm and golden brown.

Allow the pancake to set a few minutes before slicing.

Serve warm together with lingonberry jam or finely shredded green cabbage which has been flavored with lingon jam.

Crisp Waffles
Frasvåfflor

Wonderfully crisp and delicate waffles. Serve them with jam or lightly sugared berries and whipped cream or ice cream.

12 WAFFLES

1⅔ cup (400 ml) whipping cream
1¼ cup (300 ml) flour
⅓ cup (100 ml) water
⅛–¼ teaspoon salt

Whip the cream until thick. Beat together flour, water, and some of the cream until batter is completely smooth, without lumps. Let stand awhile to rise. Fold in the rest of the cream. Heat the waffle iron and fry until crisp and golden brown.

Pancake Torte garnished with cloudberry preserves and whipped cream

Egg Cake
Äggakaka

A typical provincial dish from Skåne. It may be served as a main course together with fried pork

4 PORTIONS

4 tablespoons flour
2½ cups (600 ml) milk
4 eggs
½ teaspoon salt
1 tablespoon butter, margarine, or pork fat
¾ lb. (300 g) salted pork

Mix the flour together with half the milk to a smooth batter, free of lumps. Add the remaining milk, the eggs, and the salt.

Brown the butter in a frying pan and pour the mixture into the pan. If the egg cake is going to be served with pork, fry the pork first. Remove the pork slices and strain the fat from the pork.

Do not fry at too high a temperature. Stick a knife or fork carefully into the batter a few times so that it sets evenly. Flip by turning the cake onto a cover and then frying the other side. Turn out onto a serving plate and serve hot. Place the slices of fried pork on top of the cake.

Baked Omelette
Ugnsomelett

This is a light and fluffy omelette, often called a Swedish omelette. It can be made fancier by using less flour and more eggs or simpler by only decreasing the flour. It is a good lunch or supper dish, but may also be served as a hot dish on a smörgåsbord.

1 OMELETTE

1 ⅓ cups (300 ml) milk
2 teaspoons flour
3 eggs
½ teaspoon salt
pinch white pepper
½–¾ tablespoon butter or margarine
FILLINGS:
Creamed vegetables, page 66, creamed mushrooms, or shrimp or shellfish in white sauce.

Bring the milk to a boil and allow to cool a little. Mix the flour together with a little of the milk. Beat together the eggs, flour mixture, the remaining milk, and salt and pepper in a bowl. Be sure to mix well. Pour the batter into a well greased ovenproof frying pan with sloping sides about 8″ (18 cm) in diameter or an ovenproof baking dish. Bake 20 minutes at 400°F (205°C) in middle of oven or until the omelette is golden yellow and the batter is firmly set.

Turn the omelette (if baked in frying pan) onto a warm serving platter. Pour filling on half the omelette and fold together carefully. If the omelette is baked in a baking dish, pour the filling over the entire omelette instead.

Serve together with a fresh salad or with tomatoes and cucumbers.

Desserts

Nowadays one can find rose hip soup, fruit soups and puddings, and cheescake from Små-land in supermarkets throughout Sweden. However, if you take the time to make these desserts from scratch, the result is quite another taste experience!

Don't forget the crumb pies or the lingonberry parfait-- two other Swedish desserts that are tops!

Strawberry Fruit Pudding
Jordgubbskräm

Choose juicy, well-ripened berries.

4 SERVINGS

2–3 cups (500–750 ml) fresh strawberries
2 cups (500 ml) water
¼–⅓ cup (75–100 ml) sugar
2½ tablespoons potato flour

Rinse and top the berries. If the berries are large, cut in slices or halves. Mix the berries, water, sugar, and potato flour together in a saucepan. Bring to a boil, stirring carefully.

Pour immediately into serving bowl. Sugar lightly on the surface so that a film doesn't form. Allow to cool.

Instead of strawberries one can substitute with other juicy berries, such as raspberries, blueberries, red currants, etc.

Serve the fruit pudding cooled, or chilled, together with milk.

Rose Hip Soup
Nyponsoppa

6 PORTIONS

WITH DRIED ROSE HIPS:
1¼ cups (300 ml) pitted and dried rose hips
1½ qts. (1½ liter) water
⅓ cup (100 ml) sugar
1½ tablespoons potato flour

Crush the rose hips. Soak in water a few hours. Boil 20–30 minutes in the same water until soft. Press through a strainer. If necessary, dilute the purée with enough water to make 1½ qts.

Bring the rose hip mixture and sugar to a boil. Stir the potato flour together with a little cold water until dissolved. Remove saucepan from heat and thicken by adding the flour-water mixture slowly in a thin stream, stirring constantly. Bring to a boil again. Allow to cool.

Serve together with rusks or with a dollop of ice cream or whipped cream.

4 PORTIONS

WITH ROSE HIP PURÉE:
1 tablespoon potato flour
3 cups (700 ml) water
1¼ cups (300 ml) rose hip purée
⅛–¼ cup (50–75 ml) sugar

Rose hip purée is made from fresh rose hips which are boiled and then strained.

Blend the potato flour with a little cold water. Boil the rest of the water. Remove from heat. Stir in the potato flour mixture. Add the rose hip pulp and sugar. Frozen purée doesn't need to be thawed. Sweeten to taste. Serve as above.

Fruit Salad
Fruktsallad

10 PORTIONS

5 oranges
5 apples
5 pears
3 bananas
½ cup (100 ml) coarsely chopped hazelnuts
½ cup (100 ml) raisins
4 oranges
fresh orange juice
(sugar)

Peel the oranges. Slice segments into smaller sections. Peel the apples and pears if desired. Core and slice into small pieces. Peel and slit the bananas lengthwise and then in slices.

Put fruit, raisins, and nuts in a large bowl, alternating layers.

Add a little sugar to the orange juice and pour over fruit if necessary. Cover and let stand awhile to draw.

Blend the salad carefully so that it is moist throughout. The fruit salad should not be too cold when served. Room temperature is best so the fruit flavors come to their essence.

Lingonberry Parfait
Lingonparfait

10 PORTIONS

3 egg yolks
⅓ cup (100 ml) sugar
2 cups (500 ml) fresh or frozen lingonberries
2 cups (500 ml) whipping cream

Sort and rinse the fresh berries. Thaw frozen berries.

Cream egg yolks and sugar until light and fluffy.

Purée the berries in a blender or food processor. The berries can even be mashed by hand with a potato masher. Stir the berries into the egg mixture.

Bring cream to a boil and pour over berry mixture immediately , stirring vigorously. Allow to cool.

Pour the mixture into a mould or round bowl and place in freezer overnight.

Thaw 15–30 minutes before releasing from mould.

Lemon or Orange Mousse
Citronfromage

The mousse must be made well in advance of serving. It can have different flavors with its name reflecting the flavoring used.

4 PORTIONS

5 sheets of gelatin (Calculate : 1 envelope gelatin per cup
*   of liquid)*
water
3 large eggs
⅔ cup (150 ml) sugar
grated rind of 1 lemon or orange
freshly squeezed juice from 1 lemon or 3 oranges
water

Soak the sheets of gelatin in very cold water. If using gelatin powder mix powder with sugar and eggs. Cream eggs and sugar until light and fluffy, preferably with an electric mixer. Blend in the rind and juice from the lemons or oranges. Dilute the juice with water to make 1 cup.

Squeeze water from the gelatin and melt them slowly in a saucepan over low heat. Add the gelatin, pouring in a steady stream, to the egg mixture, beating constantly. Pour into a bowl. Refrigerate for about 3 hours until firm.

Substitute citrus fruit for 1 cup fresh, crushed berries.

Rhubarb Crumb Pie

Rhubarb Crumb Pie
Smulpaj med rabarber

4–6 PORTIONS

¾ cups (200 ml) flour
2–3 tablespoons sugar
¼ cup (50 ml) chopped almonds or nuts (optional)
⅓ cup (75 g) butter or margarine
FILLING:
⅔ lb. (400 g) rhubarb
⅓ cup (100 ml) sugar
1 tablespoon potato flour

Blend flour, sugar, and nuts (optional) in a bowl or food processor. Break butter into smaller pieces and add to flour mixture. Mix until crust is coarse and crumbly.

Rinse the rhubarb. Remove any tough peel. Slice into 1″ long pieces. Mix with sugar and potato flour. Alternate the rhubarb with the sugar and flour mixture in layers in an ovenproof dish.

Spread the crumb crust on top.

Bake at 435°F (225°C) in the center of the oven for about 30 minutes or until the rhubarb is tender and the pie has a golden color.

Serve with vanilla sauce, whipped cream, or ice cream.

Swedish Applesauce Cake
Svensk äppelkaka

4 PORTIONS

4–5 tart apples (approximately 1 lb./500 g)
water
sugar
1¼ cups (300 ml) coarsely ground rusks
2–3 tablespoons butter or margarine
1 teaspoon ground cinnamon
sugar
(powdered sugar)

Peel, core, and cut the apples into large slices. Boil in a little water until they become soft and mushy. Sugar to taste.

Brown the ground rusks in butter together with a little sugar and the cinnamon.

Grease an ovenproof baking dish or skillet. Spread a layer of crushed rusks on the bottom of the baking dish and then alternate with layers of applesauce and rusks, the top layer being crushed rusks.

Bake in the center of the oven about 30 minutes at 435°F (225°C). Cool completely in baking dish. Tip carefully onto a serving platter.

Garnish with powdered sugar if desired. Place narrow strips of paper in a checkerboard pattern on the cake and sprinkle with a thin layer of powdered sugar. Remove the strips.

Serve with vanilla custard.

Cheesecake from Småland
Småländsk ostkaka

6–8 PORTIONS

5¾ qts. (6 liter) milk
⅔ cup (150 ml) flour
2 teaspoons rennet
2 cups (500 ml) coffee cream (half and half)
  or 1⅓ cups (300 ml) whipping cream or ¾ cup
  (200 ml) milk
⅓ cup (75 ml) sugar

3 eggs
2 oz. (50 g) blanched sweet almonds, chopped
4 blanched bitter almonds, chopped

Heat the milk to 95°F (35°C). Remove the saucepan from the heat and sift in the flour while beating. Stir rennet into mixture and allow to stand until it curdles. Stir now and then so that the whey separates.

Strain the curd thoroughly through a strainer or cheesecloth.

Beat together the cream, sugar, eggs, and almonds and mix with the curd Pour into a 1 qt. greased oven-proof baking dish. Bake in lower part of oven for about one hour at 350°F (175°C), preferably over a water-bath. The water-bath can be omitted; however the cheesecake will then have another consistency.

Serve the cheesecake lukewarm, or chilled, together with a good jam or compote.

Rice à la Malta
Ris à la Malta

A classic dessert which can be made from new boiled rice or from leftover rice pudding.

4 PORTIONS

⅔ cup (150 ml) long-grained rice
water
salt
¾ cup (200 ml) whipping cream
1–2 tablespoons sugar
2–3 teaspoons vanilla essence (1–2 tablespoons vanilla sugar)

Boil the rice according to package directions. Rinse in cold water and allow to drain well.

Beat the cream until thick and flavor with sugar and vanilla. Blend the rice into the cream mixture. Pour into a large bowl and refrigerate.

2 cups boiled rice pudding can be substituted for the long-grained rice, water, and salt.

Serve the rice cold together with fresh berry preserves, jam, compote, or fruit sauce.

Swedish Rice Pudding

Swedish Rice Pudding
Risgrynsgröt

Rice pudding is the classical Christmas dessert but can be eaten at other times as well. It can be made fancier by mixing it together with whipped cream. Long or round-grained rice can be used. Rice pudding made with long-grained rice is white and fluffy.

4 PORTIONS

⅔ cup (150 ml) long or round-grained rice
1⅓ cups (300 ml) water
½–1 teaspoon salt
1 cinnamon stick (optional)
3–3½ cups (700–800 ml) milk
1–2 tablespoons sugar
⅓ cup (100 ml) whipping cream

Stir together the rice, water, and salt in a saucepan. Add optional cinnamon stick.

Cover and boil on low heat about 10 minutes. Dilute with milk and stir.

Bring rice to boil again and let swell, covered, on very low heat for about 40 minutes. Do not stir until rice is completely cooked.

If desired, one can flavor with sugar and fold whipped cream gently into the pudding.

Breads and Baked Goods

Some allege that Sweden is mostly known for its rye bread and crisp flatbread. Nothing could be farther from the truth – Swedish cuisine includes a great variety of breads, even from a historical perspective. For example, in Bohuslän, on the West Coast, wives of seamen baked a special type of bread called hönökaka that kept well on their long sea journies. In the northernmost provinces one baked flatbread. Skåne was known for its moist rye bread which was prepared employing a special technique that used scalding water to soften the hull of the grain.

Here follows a delicious collection of tasty buns, cookies and cakes, including Christmas specialities such as almond tarts, ginger snaps, and crullers. Princess cake, the all-time favorite of Swedes, is also included.

Hönö Bread
Hönökakor

There are many variations of this bread which is often baked on the islands off the West Coast of Sweden.

8–10 ROUNDS OF BREAD

2 oz. (50 g) active compressed yeast
½ cup (100 g) butter of margarine
1 qt. (1 liter) milk
¼ cup (50 ml) light corn syrup
3 teaspoons salt
3 teaspoons ground aniseed
3 teaspoons ground fennel
2 cups (500 ml) rye flour
8 cups (2 liters) all-purpose flour (approximately)

Crumble the yeast in a mixing bowl. In saucepan melt the butter and then add the milk. Heat to 99°F (37°C) or lukewarm. Dissolve the yeast in a little of the warm milk. Add the rest of the liquid , syrup, salt, aniseed, fennel, and rye flour to the yeast. Stir together and add the all-purpose flour. Work the dough until smooth and shiny. Cover and let rise 20–30 minutes.

Turn the dough out onto a floured surface and knead well. Divide into 8–10 sections and roll each section into a smooth ball. Cover and let rise under a baking cloth in a warm room 25–30 minutes. Then, with a rolling pin, roll out large rounds of bread, about 10″ (27 cm) in diameter.

Place bread on a greased baking sheet and allow to rise 5 minutes. Prick surface with fork. Bake in the center of the oven for about 5 minutes. Cover and let cool.

Soft Flatbread
Mjukt tunnbröd

14 ROUNDS OF FLATBREAD

½ oz. active compressed yeast (14 g)
¼ cup (50 g) butter or margarine
2½ cups (500 ml) milk
½ teaspoon salt
¼ cup (50 ml) sugar
2 tablespoons light corn syrup
½ teaspoon ammonium carbonate
½ cup (150 ml) graham flour (full-measure)
¾ cup (200 ml) rye flour
2¾ (700 ml) cups all-purpose flour, plus additional flour
* for baking*

Soft Flatbread

Crumble yeast in a mixing bowl. Melt butter. Add milk and warm until lukewarm 99°F (37°C).

Dissolve the yeast in a little of the milk mixture. Add the rest of the liquid, salt, sugar, syrup, ammonium carbonate, graham flour, and rye flour to the yeast mixture. Work in the flour. Cover and let rise for about 45 minutes. Turn out onto a floured surface.

Divide the dough, which shouldn't be too stiff, into 14 round balls. Roll out very thin (½ cm or ⅛″ thick), preferably using a rippled rolling pin. Wrap the thin dough around the rolling pin and brush away any extra flour.

Carefully place the bread on the stove in a heated frying. Fry about 2 minutes on each side over medium heat.

Place on a cooling rack, cover, and allow to cool.

Brogårds Bread
Brogårdskakor

Brogårds Bread is a thin type of flatbread.

40 ROUND CAKES

1 oz. (about 25 g) active compressed yeast
2 cups (500 ml) water
1 teaspoon salt
½ tablespon crushed fennel
½ tablespoon crushed aniseed
4 cups (1 liter) fine rye flour
¾ cup (200 ml) all-purpose flour

Crumble yeast in a mixing bowl. Heat water to 99°F (37°C). Dissolve yeast in a little of the water and then add the remaining water, salt, and spices. Mix together with half the rye flour and work the dough a couple of minutes. Add the remaining flour, saving ½ cup for baking. The dough should be rather soft. Sprinkle with a little flour, cover, and let rise until double.

Turn the dough out onto a floured surface. Knead and divide into 40 pieces. Form into balls. Roll out in rye flour to circular thin rounds. Place on greased baking sheets. Make a hole in the middle of each round. Allow to rise about 10 minutes.

Bake at 435°F (225°C) for 4–5 minutes in the center of the oven.. Cool, uncovered, on rack. The bread can be threaded on a stick and will then keep for several weeks.

Skåne Loaf
Skånelimpa

Tasty rye bread, also known as "Skåne Kavring". The dough can be spiced with 1½–2 teaspoons of ground or crushed caraway. Best results are attained by kneading a stiff dough very thoroughly.

2 LOAVES

DAY 1:
1 qt (1 liter) water
6 cups (1½ liter) coarse rye flour
DAY 2:
2⅔ oz. (75 g) active compressed yeast
1 teaspoon salt
⅓ cup (100 ml) buttermilk or 1 teaspoon vinegar essence
¼ cup (50 ml) corn syrup
4 cups (1 liter) all-purpose flour (approximately)
GARNISH:
warm water

Pour hot water over the rye flour and blend together well. Cover and let stand over-night.

The next day, add the crumbled yeast, salt, buttermilk or vinegar essence, and syrup. Let the dough rise for 30 minutes and then work the all-purpose flour into the dough until it is firm. Knead well and divide into two even halves. Make two smooth loaves, prick with a fork, and place on a greased baking sheet.

Allow to rise until almost double in size. Bake 1½ hours in lower part of oven at 350°F (175°C). Brush with warm water just before removing bread from oven. Wrap in cloth and allow to cool.

Skåne Loaf

Sweet Yeast Bread
Vetebröd

Sweet yeast bread is one of the most common forms of coffee bread. It can be made into either loaves or buns.

36–40 COFFEE ROLLS OR 3 LOAVES

BASIC YEAST BREAD DOUGH RECIPE:
½ cup (100 g) margarine or butter
2 cups (500 ml) milk
2 oz. (50 g) active compressed yeast
½ teaspoon salt
½–¾ cup (100–150 ml) sugar
1 teaspoon cardamom
5–6 cups (1,3 liter) all-purpose flour

CINNAMON AND SUGAR FILLING:
½ cup (100 g) margarine or butter
⅓ cup (100 ml) sugar
2 teaspoons ground cinnamon

ALMOND FILLING:
⅔ lb. (150 g) grated almond paste or marzipan
¼ cup (50 g) sugar
2 teaspoons freshly crushed cardamom seeds

TOPPING AND DECORATION:
1 egg
crushed nib sugar, chopped sweet almonds

Melt the butter or margarine. Add the milk and warm until lukewarm.

Crumble the yeast in a small bowl. Dissolve yeast in a little of the milk mixture. Pour in the rest of the liquid, salt, sugar, ground cardamom seeds, and about ⅔ of the flour. Work until smooth and shiny, by machine or by hand. Add more flour, but save some for rolling out the dough. The dough is ready when it loosens from the sides of the bowl. Sprinkle a little flour over the bowl. Cover and let to rise until double in size in a draft-free place.

Knead the dough a few minutes in the bowl. Remove from bowl and place on floured surface. Knead with the remaining flour until dough is ready (no longer sticks to the baking surface or hands).

COFFEE ROLLS: Make flat, round or filled rolls. Place on greased baking sheets. Cover and let rise until double in size.

Brush with beaten egg. Decorate with nib sugar and almonds if desired.

Bake at 475°F (250°C) for 5–10 minutes in the center of the oven.

LOAVES OF COFFEE BREAD: (3 loaves). Make basic bread dough, but knead in an extra ½–¾ cup flour.

Divide into three equal sections.

Roll out each piece to a 8″×10″ (20×35 cm) rectangular. Spread one of the fillings on top. Roll together starting from the long side. Place roll on greased baking sheet. Using scissors, cut gashes across the top of the loaf either in a herringbone pattern or towards each other from the far ends.

Place the loaves on greased baking sheets, but not so close that they touch and lose their shape while rising. Cover and let rise at room temperature for 20–30 minutes.

Brush with beaten egg or milk. Sprinkle nib sugar and/or almonds on top if desired.

Bake in lower part of oven for 15–20 minutes at 400–435°F (200–225°C). Cover loaves while cooling so they remain moist.

Shrove Tuesday Buns
Semlor

The word "semla" comes from the Latin simila, which simply means "finely sifted white flour". From the beginning, these buns were an expensive delicacy, filled with almonds and garnished with rich cream. The name, Shrove Tuesday Buns, refers to the time of year, traditionally, when they are eaten. Many eat these buns together with warm milk.

10–12 BUNS

⅓ cup (75 g) butter or margarine
1¼ cups (300 ml) milk
2 oz. (50 g) active compressed yeast
½ teaspoon salt
⅓ cup (100 ml) sugar
1 egg
½ teaspoon ammonium carbonate
4 cups (900 ml) all-purpose flour (approximately)

Shrove Tuesday Buns

1 beaten egg, for brushing dough
FILLING:
½ cup (100 g) sweet almonds
½ cup (100 ml) sugar
½ cup (100 ml) milk or cream
bread from inside the roll
GARNISH:
¾ cup (200 ml) whipping cream
1 tablespoon powdered sugar

Melt the butter and add the milk. Let mixture stand until lukewarm or 99°F (37°C). Dissolve yeast in some of the milk mixture. Add the rest of the liquid, salt, sugar, and egg. Mix the ammonium carbonate with some of the flour and add to liquid mixture. Mix in enough flour so that the dough is pliable, using a machine or working by hand. It should loosen from the sides of the bowl. Cover and let rise until almost double, about 20–30 minutes.

Turn out the dough onto a floured surface and knead until smooth, using the remaining flour. Shape into 10–12 round balls. Place on greased baking sheet, cover, and let rise about 20 minutes. Brush with the beaten egg.

Bake the buns in the center of the oven for 5–10 minutes at 475°F (250°C). Remove from oven, cover with a baking cloth and cool.

Scald, peel, and grind the almonds. Slice a lid off the top of each bun and make a large well in the center of the bun. Make filling by mixing the bread taken from the buns together with the almonds, sugar, and milk or cream. The filling should be thin. Refill each well with the almond filling and decorate with whipped cream. Replace the lids and garnish with powdered sugar sprinkled on top.

Saffron Buns
Saffransbröd

These delicious golden buns are baked for Christmas and to celebrate Lucia. They are shaped into many different figures, with each province being represented by its own particular shape previously. By mixing an egg into the dough, it will become easier to handle. One can either garnish the buns with raisins or work them into the dough instead.

30 BUNS

⅔ cup (175 g) butter or margarine
2 cups (500 ml) milk
2 oz. (50 g) active compressed yeast
¼ teaspoon salt
¾ cup (175 ml) sugar
0.20 oz. (1g) grains of saffron
1 egg (optional)
½ cup (100 ml) raisins
6–6½ cups (1½ liter) all-purpose flour
1 egg, for brushing the buns before baking

Melt butter and pour in milk. Heat mixture to 99°F (37°C) or lukewarm.

Dissolve crumbled yeast into milk mixture. Add rest of liquid, salt, sugar, saffron, egg and raisins as well, if desired. Using a machine, or by hand, work in as much flour as necessary to form a soft dough that is easy to handle and loosens from the sides of the mixing bowl.

Sprinkle a little flour over the dough; cover with a baking cloth and let rise in a warm place for about 30 minutes.

Knead the dough in the bowl for a few minutes. Turn dough out onto a floured surface. Knead until smooth and shiny.

Form into different shapes ("lussekatter") by breaking off pieces of dough and making ½″ strips with which to work. Garnish with raisins, if desired.

Put onto a greased baking sheet. Cover and let rise until double in size, approximately 30 minutes. Brush buns with a beaten egg. Bake at 435–475°F (225–250°C) for 5–10 minutes in the center of the oven. Remove from oven. Cover and let buns cool.

Quick Rolls
Hastbullar

These are quick and easy to stir together while the oven heats.

20–25 ROLLS

2 cups (500 ml) flour
½ cup (100 ml) sugar
2 teaspoons baking powder
2 teaspoons crushed cardamom
⅓ cup (75–100 g) butter or margarine
1 egg
¾ cup (200 ml) milk or buttermilk
½ cup (100 ml) raisins
2 tablespoons candied orange peel
TOPPING:
1 egg
nib sugar

Mix together all the dry ingredients in a bowl. Cut together the flour and butter with fingers until coarsely blended. Quickly stir the egg and milk into mixture to form a dough. Do not overstir or the dough becomes tough.

Stir in the raisins and candied orange peel.

Drop by rounded spoonfuls into cupcake forms. Place on baking sheets. Brush rolls with the beaten egg and sprinkle with nib sugar.

Bake at about 425–435°F (220–250°C) for 10 minutes in the center of the oven.

Saffron Buns

Danish Pastry
Wienerbröd

The secret of "flaky" and crisp Danish pastry is the generous slices of margarine that are rolled into the yeast dough. Margarine is easier to slice than butter. It is an art to be able to handle Danish pastry dough, so don't give up if the results aren't perfect the first time! All ingredients should be placed in the refrigerator well before starting, and the kitchen should be cool. Baking Danish pastry on a warm summer day is almost impossible.

2 LARGE RECTANGLES

2 oz. (50 g) active compressed yeast
1 cup (250 ml) milk
⅛ teaspoon salt
1½ tablespoons sugar
1 egg
3⅓ cups (800 ml) all-purpose flour, approximately
1–1⅓ cups (250–300 g) margarine
NUT FILLING:
¼ cup (50 g) nuts
¼ cup (50 g) butter or margarine
¼ cup (75 ml) sugar
VANILLA CUSTARD:
1 cup (250 ml) milk
2 tablespoons flour
2 egg yolks or 1 egg
1 tablespoon sugar
2 teaspoons vanilla sugar or 1 teaspoon vanilla essence
TOPPING:
1 egg
GLAZE:
⅓–½ cup (100 ml) powdered sugar
¾ tablespoon water

Dissolve the yeast in the cold milk. Add salt, sugar, and beaten egg. Stir in enough flour so that the dough is easy to handle. Turn dough onto a lightly-floured surface and knead until smooth , using a little additional flour. Save about ½ cup of flour for later use.

Roll out the dough and fold it in half. Roll it out again to form ½" (1 cm) thick rectangle, 12"×15"
(30×40 cm) in size. Place thin slices of margarine over ⅔ of the dough. Fold into thirds, starting with the fat-free section. Turn the folded dough a quarter way around. Lightly pound the dough in both directions on a floured surface to make a rectangle once more. Again, fold the dough in thirds. Chill and let rest for about 10 minutes. Repeat this procedure twice. Make one of the following fillings:

NUT FILLING: Grind or finely chop the nuts. Cream the butter and sugar until smooth and add the nuts.

VANILLA CUSTARD: Beat together milk, flour, egg yolks or egg, and sugar in a saucepan. Simmer, stirring constantly until mixture reaches custard consistency. Cool and add vanilla.

BAKING: Roll out dough to form a ½" (1 cm) thick rectangle, 15"×23" (40×60 cm) in size. Divide rectangle in half lengthwise. Put a strip of vanilla custard or nut filling down the middle of the dough. Pinch the edges so that they don't start to leaven in the oven. Place on baking sheets and let rise 1–1½ hours.

Brush the pastry with a beaten egg. Bake in lower part of oven for 15–20 minutes at 435–450°F (225–230°C). Remove from oven. Leave pastry on baking sheets a few minutes before transfering to cooling racks. Cool under baking cloth. Make a thin glaze by mixing together powdered sugar and water. Drizzle on pastry.

Danish pastry is a perfect refrigerator bread. Chill the dough overnight, allowing it to rise slowly, and bake the following morning.

Hot Sponge Cake
Sockerkaka

I CAKE

¼ cup (50 g) butter or margarine
2 eggs
¾ cup (200 ml) sugar
1¼ cups (300 ml) all-purpose flour
2 teaspoons baking powder
⅓ cup (100 ml) milk
finely grated peel from ½ lemon
PREPARE THE BAKING FORM:
butter or margarine
bread crumbs

Grease and bread a 1½ qt. rectangular or round baking pan.

Melt the margarine or butter and let it cool to room temperature or let it stand in room temperature until soft and pliable.

Cream eggs and sugar until light and fluffy.

Mix together the flour, baking powder, and lemon peel and add to the egg mixture. Blend well and beat until the dough is smooth and even. Add milk mixture mix well, and pour into prepared baking form. Bake on a rack in the lower part of the oven for about 35 minutes at 350°F (175°C). Let cool in form several minutes before turning upside down on a rack.

Cover with a baking cloth and allow to cool.

Instead of lemon peel one can substitute either orange peel or 2 teaspoons vanilla.

Fyris Apple Cake
Fyriskaka

I CAKE

¾ cup (200 g) butter
1 cup (250 ml) sugar
3 eggs
1⅔ cups (400 ml) flour
1 teaspoon baking powder
⅓ cup (100 ml) milk or cream
grated lemon peel from ½ lemon
TOPPING:
3–4 apples
1–2 tablespoon sugar
1 teaspoons ground cinnamon

Cream butter and sugar until light, preferably with an electric beater. Add eggs, one at a time, beating constantly. The batter canl be grainy, but will become smooth when flour is added. Flavor with the lemon.

Mix together the flour and baking powder. Blend dry ingredients with the batter and mix until smooth. Add the milk or cream. Pour the batter in a greased and breaded 10″ (24 cm) baking form, preferably a spring form.

Peel and core apples. Cut into slices. Press apple slices into the batter. Mix cinnamon and sugar together and sprinkle over the batter.

Bake at 350°F (175°C) for 45–50 minutes on a rack in the lower part of oven.

Cool a little before before removing from form and place on cooling rack.

Serve in slices together with softened ice cream or as a cake topped with whipped cream.

Swedish Gingerbread
Mjuk pepparkaka

I CAKE

½ cup (100 g) butter or margarine (full measure)
2 eggs
¾ cup (225 ml) sugar
⅔ cup (150 ml) sour cream
1½ teaspoon ginger
1½ teaspoon cloves
2 teaspoons cinnamon
1¼ cups (275 ml) all-purpose flour
1 teaspoon baking soda or 2 teaspoons baking powder

Grease and bread a 1½ qt. (1½ liter) bread pan or cake pan.

Melt butter and allow to cool.

Cream eggs and sugar until light and fluffy. Add the sour cream, butter, and flour mixed with baking soda or baking powder. Pour batter into form.

Bake in lower part of oven for about 45 minutes at 400°F (200°C).

Almond Tarts
Mandelmusslor

ABOUT 50 TARTS

¾ cup (200 ml) sweet almonds
4–5 bitter almonds
a little less than 1 cup (200 g) butter or margarine
½ cup (150 ml) sugar (full measure)
1 egg
1⅓ cups flour

Blanche, peel, and grind the almonds.

Cream butter and sugar. Add the almonds, egg, and most of the flour. Knead on a lightly-floured surface together with the remaining flour. Wrap in plastic wrap and chill for at least one hour in the refrigerator.

Shape the dough into a long small roll. Slice in sections and press into greased fluted tart forms. Place on a baking sheet.

Bake at 400°F (200°C) for about 8 minutes in the center of the oven. Remove from forms immediately.

Swedish Gingersnaps
Pepparkakor

Swedish ginger snaps are baked at Christmas and are served with either glögg or coffee.

150 COOKIES

1⅓ cups (300 ml) sugar
¼ cup (50 ml) corn syrup
⅓ cup (100 ml) water
a little less than 1 cup of butter or margarine (200 g)
1 tablespoon ground bitter orange peel
1–2 tablespoons ground cinnamon
½ tablespoon ground ginger
½ tablespoon ground cloves
2 teaspoons finely-crushed cardamom seeds
2 teaspoons baking soda
4 cups (1 liter) all-purpose flour (approximately)
sweet almonds (optional)

Boil sugar, syrup, and water together in a saucepan.

Put the butter and spices in a large mixing bowl. Pour in the hot sugar mixture. Stir until the butter has melted. Allow to cool.

Blend baking soda together with most of the flour.

Quickly mix the ingredients to a smooth dough. Cover and let stand overnight.

Roll out a portion of the dough at a time. Do not press the dough hard. Roll out the dough, lightly, with a rolling pin instead.

Cut out shapes from the dough with cookie cutters. Round cookies can be decorated with blanched almond halves.

Place the cookies on cold, greased cookie sheets.

Bake the cookies at 400–430°F (200–220°C) for about 5–8 minutes in the center of the oven. Check the cookies while baking, as they burn easily!

Swedish Gingersnaps

Lace Oatmeal Wafers
Havreflam

25–30 WAFERS

⅓ cup (75 g) butter or margarine
1 cup (250 ml) oatmeal
½ cup (125 ml) sugar (full-measure)
1 egg
5–6 bitter almonds
1 tablespoon all-purpose flour
1 teaspoon baking powder

Melt the butter or margarine and pour over the oat-meal immediately. Allow mixture to cool.

Stir in sugar, the lightly-beaten egg, grated or ground almonds, and the flour mixed with the baking powder.

Drop the dough by spoonfuls onto a greased baking sheet. Place only 6–8 spoonfuls on each sheet, as the batter spreads out while baking.

Bake at 430°F (220°C) for about 6 minutes in the center of the oven.

Princess Torte
Prinsesstårta

20 SLICES

4 eggs
¾ cup full measure (200 ml) sugar
½ cup (100 ml) all-purpose flour
⅓ cup (100 ml) potato flour
2 teaspoon baking powder
FILLING:
1¼ cups (300 ml) vanilla custard
2 tablespoons sugar
1⅔ cups (450 ml) whipping cream
TOPPING:
¾ lb. (400 g) marzipan
1¼ cups (300 ml) powdered sugar
1 tablespoon glucose
green food coloring
powdered sugar, sifted

Grease and bread a high round cake pan, about 9″ (22 cm) in diameter.

Cream the eggs and sugar until light. Mix together the flours and baking powder. Fold into the creamed mixture. Pour into cake pan.

Place the pan on a rack in the lower part of the oven and bake at 350°F (175°C) about 40 minutes. Remove from oven and allow cake to cool in pan several minutes before turning out on cooling rack.

When cool, split the cake into three layers. The top layer should be less than 1/3″ (1 cm) thick.

Make the vanilla custard and flavor with sugar.

Beat the cream until stiff and fold into the vanilla custard. Spread part of the filling, in mounds, between the layers, saving enough to frost the tops and sides of the cake. Store frosted cake in a cool place.

Work together the marzipan and powdered sugar until smooth. Add food coloring and blend well until the marzipan is pale green in color. Roll out between pieces of plastic wrap until you have made a thin flat circle, large enough to cover the entire cake. Trim the edges. Place the marzipan cover carefully over the top of the cake. Use leftover strips of marzipan to decorate the bake.

Using a flour sifter or sieve, sprinkle powdered sugar over the cake.

Keep cool until serving.

Swedish Whipped Cream Cake
Gräddtårta

Using different combinations of fruits and berries, this classic cake offers an almost infinite number of variations.

10–12 SLICES

4 eggs
¾ cups full measure (200 ml) sugar
½ cup (100 ml) flour
¼ cup (75 ml) potato flour
1½ teaspoons baking powder
FILLING:
¾ cup (200 ml) whipping cream
berries and fruits of different sorts
DECORATION:
1¼ cups (300 ml) whipping cream
berries or fruits as in filling
walnuts, chopped nuts, or grated chocolate

Grease and line a large (3 qt.) cake pan with fine dried bread crumbs.

Cream butter and sugar until light. Mix together flour, potato flour, and baking powder separately and then mix together with egg mixture. Pour into cake pan. Bake at 350°F (175°C) for 40 minutes in lower part of oven. Remove cake from the pan and let cool. Split into three layers.

Whip the cream stiff. Put aside half the whipped cream for decorating the top layer. Put the cake layers together, filling each layer with whipped cream and crushed or sliced berries. Frost the tops and sides of the cake with the remaining whipped cream. Decorate with fruit and/or berries, nuts, or grated chocolate.

Swedish Whipped Cream Cake

Wheat Rusks
Veteskorpor

ABOUT 100 PIECES

1 cup (250 g) butter or margarine (full measure)
2 cups (500 ml) milk
2 oz. (50 g) active compressed yeast
½ teaspoon salt
⅔ cup (150 ml) sugar
1 tablespoon ground cardamom
6 cups (1½ liter) all-purpose flour (approximately)

Melt butter in a saucepan and pour in milk. Cool to lukewarm.

Dissolve the yeast in a little of the milk mixture. Add the rest of the milk mixture, salt, sugar, and cardamom. Work in enough of the flour so that the dough is smooth and loosens from the sides of the bowl. Sprinkle with a little flour. Cover and let rise for about 30 minutes.

Turn out dough onto a floured surface and knead until smooth using the remaining flour. The dough should be quite soft and "rich". Divide into quarters that are smooth and about 16″ (40 cm) long. Place onto greased baking sheets. Cover and let rise 30–40 minutes.

Bake at 435°F (225°C) for 15–20 minutes in the center of the oven.

Slice the cooled lengths into sections about 1¼″ (3 cm) wide. Split in half and toast the topsides at 435°F (225°C). Dry the rusks at 165–210°F (75–100°C) or in the after-heat from the oven.

Swedish Crullers
Klenäter

These are classic Swedish Christmas cookies which can be enjoyed together with a cup of coffee or as a dessert with jam and whipped cream. For best results the dough should be chilled overnight before frying.

ABOUT 50 CRULLERS

¼ cup (50 g) butter or margarine
5 egg yolks
4 tablespoons sugar
grated peel of ½ lemon
1 tablespoon aquavit or brandy
1⅓ cups (325 ml) all-purpose flour (approximately)
TO FRY:
oil
GARNISH:
sugar (optional)

Melt the butter or margarine and allow to cool.

Cream the egg yolks and sugar. Add the cooled melted butter, lemon peel, optional aquavit or brandy, and flour and mix until dough is smooth. Wrap dough in aluminum foil and chill several hours, preferably overnight.

Roll out the dough as thin as possible on a lightly floured surface. Using a pastry wheel, cut the dough into strips (1½″ (3 cm) wide and 4″ (10 cm) long. Make a slit in the center of each strip, and draw one end of the dough through the slit. Place on a cutting board and let rest awhile so that the dough becomes a little dry.

Heat the oil in a saucepan or cast-iron frying pan with straight sides. To test the temperature of the oil, use candy thermometer. The oil is ready when the thermometer reaches 365°F (185°C) or when a small piece of dry, white bread begins to dance about (and turn gold after about a minute) when dropped into the oil. Be careful that the oil doesn't become too hot. For safety's sake keep a large lid nearby to help extinguish any fire that might occur.

Place a few crullers at a time in the hot oil. Fry until golden brown. Drain on paper towels. If desired, dip in sugar.

Beverages

Gunnel's Glögg
Gunnels glögg

ABOUT 1½ QUARTS

1 bottle (75 cl) purchased wine glögg
1 bottle (75 cl) ordinary red wine
1–2 sticks of cinnamon
5 whole cloves
1 piece ginger
SERVED TOGETHER WITH:
blanched sweet almonds
raisins

Stir together the ingredients in a kettle and let stand for several hours.

Heat and serve in mugs. If desired, put a few blanched almonds and raisins in the bottom of the mug before filling with glögg.

Black Currant Glögg
Svart vinbärsglögg

ABOUT 1 QUART

¾ cup (200 ml) apple juice
1½ cups (400 ml) black currant fruit syrup
  (or juice that has been thickened to syrup consistency)
1½ (400 ml) cups water
1 teaspoon cardamom seeds
1 cinnamon stick
4 whole cloves
TO BE SERVED WITH:
½ cup (150 ml) blanched sweet almonds
½ cup (150 ml) raisins

Stir the ingredients together in a large saucepan and bring to a boil. Let stand in a cool place overnight.

Strain spices and reheat the glögg.

Serve in mugs together with almonds and raisins.

Make your own glögg
Bränn din egen glögg

ABOUT 1 QUART

1 bottle (75 cl) ordinary red wine
1 teaspoon cardamom seeds
5 whole cloves
1 cinnamon stick
1 piece bitter orange peel
1 large piece ginger
1¼–1¾ lbs. (300–400 g) of lump sugar
½ bottle (37 cl) unflavored aquavit or vodka
½ cup (100 ml) raisins
½ cup (100 ml) blanched sweet almonds

Stir the spices and wine together in a large saucepan. Heat slowly.

Put the sugar lumps in a sieve and place over one side of the saucepan.

Pour the alcohol into the heated wine and light with a match. Be careful of your face and hair, as the alcohol can flame up. Ladle the burning glögg over the sugar, allowing it to melt slowly. When about half the sugar has melted, cover the saucepan with a lid to extinguish the flame. Taste to see if the glögg is sweet enough. If not, light the fire again and add more melted sugar until taste is satisfactory.

After the glögg is sweetened, add raisins and almonds. Warm the glögg and ladle into mugs.

Roslagen's Coffee
Roslagskaffe

According to tradition, a coffee spoon was placed in the cup together with the coffee. When the bowl of the spoon became visible, the coffee had then attained the right strength.

I CUP

½ cup (150 ml) strong hot coffee
aquavit to taste

Pour the coffee into a cup. Spike with aquavit to taste.

Lingonberry Drink
Lingondricka

3 QUARTS

6½ qts. (6 liter) cleaned lingonberries
1½ qts. (1½ liter) water
4 teaspoons citric acid
1¼–2 cups (300–500 ml) sugar per quart strained fruit juice

Rinse the berries and mash them. Put the mashed berries in a large jug and pour the water over the fruit. Add citric acid. Cover the jug and allow to stand in a cool place 1–2 days. Stir occasionally.

Strain the juice, measure it, and add sugar. Stir until the sugar is completely dissolved. Skim and pour the lingonberry drink into sterilized bottles that have been allowed to cool. Seal immediately.

TABLE DRINK: Dilute with water to taste and serve chilled.

Swedish Culinary Glossary from A to Ö

This glossary explains a little about some of the classical Swedish dishes, many special ingredients, and a little about Swedish food traditions. You will also find a translation for some grocery items that are typically Swedish.

aladåb (à la daube): cold fish, egg, meat, or vegetables dishes in aspic.
ansjovisfiléer: Brisling anchovies fillets.

bakpulver: baking powder.
biff à la Lindström: a Russian-inspired dish made from ground beef and named after Captain Henrik Lindström, 1831–1910, who was, among other things, Russian consul in Visby.
biff à la Rydberg: a Swedish speciality named after Hotel Rydberg in Stockholm.
bitsocker: lump sugar.
blanklax: older terminology for Baltic or Atlantic salmon.
bondomelett: a simple omelette that contains onion, potatoes, salted or smoked fish or boiled ham.
bondsås: milk-based onion sauce. Often served together with fried salt herring and pork.
bruna bönor: boiled brown beans
brunkål: a speciality from Skåne made from cabbage browned in a fry pan.
brynt smör: Melt butter or margarine that has browned, but not burned, in a fry pan.
brännvinsbord: the forerunner of the smorgasbord. Long ago, dinner commenced with the "brännvinsbord" which consisted of several different sorts of schnapps, pickled herring or anchovies (vassbruk), homemade cheese, bread , and salted pretzels.
böckling: smoked Baltic herring.
bönvälling or bondbönsoppa: an old-fashioned Swedish soup that has been thickened and is made from broad beans (also called horsebeans or Jeruselem's Thorn)

citronmeliss: (hjärtansfröjd), a perennial herb with heart-shaped leaves that taste of lemon. Cultivated in Scandinavia. Used in salads but can also be mixed together with other herbs or as a garnish for desserts and beverages.

dopp i gryta, doppa: well-seasoned stock from ham, brawn, or sausage that has been reduced. Part of the Christmas smorgasbord where one dips a slice of wort bread quickly into the stock. Served together with slices of Christmas ham or brawn.
doppsko: creamed "pytt i panna" (Swedish hash). Pour cream over the hash and let it absorb into the mixture while cooking. Calculate ½–⅔ cup cream for four portions.

farinsocker: (dark brown sugar, raw sugar) less refined sugar with a somewhat spicy taste. Mostly used in baking.
fattiga riddare: simple desssert that is somewhat international. Dip slices of bread into a pancake-like batter seasoned to taste. Fry lightly on both sides and serve with sugar and perhaps a little jam.
femöring: a small serving of fillet of beef served with onions and a fried egg.
filmjölk: processed sour milk that has a consistency similar to yoghurt.
fiskbullar: fish balls.
fjärilskotlett: boneless butterfly cut of meat.
fläskhare: boneless loin of pork.
fladensill: small, oily herring found in the North Sea.
florsocker: powdered sugar

flötgröt, sammetgröt: porridge made from flour and cream. A speciality of Norrland and Norway.
franskbröd: a large loaf of French bread.
frikadeller: small boiled meatballs made from ground veal, beef, or game. Often served as a garnish with soups.
frikassé (fr): a stew or ragout of light meat.
fyra kryddor: mixture of following spices: grated nutmeg, ground white pepper, allspice, and cloves.
fårfiol: salted,dried, and smoked leg of lamb.
förlorade ägg, pocherade (fr): poached egg.

gaffelbit: bite-sized, often bite-sized pieces of pickled herring in a spicy pickling solution.
giftas: old-fashioned dessert composed of cake and rusks crumbs and whipped cream. Sometimes served together with jam or applesauce.
glasmästarsill: herring pickled together with root vegetables, onion, and spices.
glödhoppa: thin slices of salted or smoked lamb meat (usually) that are barbequed or slightly broiled. A speciality from Gotland.
grahamsbröd: wholewheat bread.
grava: old-fashioned method for preservation, still very prevalent, mainly used for fish. Fish fillets are rubbed with a mixture of salt, sugar, and spices. Should stand in a cool place from 1–3 days.
grevé: a round, porous, Swedish hard cheese that resembles swiss cheese, and has a mild sweet nutty flavor.
grädde: cream.
gräddfil: sour cream.
gubbröra: A fried mixture consisting of chopped anchovies, onion, eggs, and parsley. Served as an appetizer, lunch, or late night supper.

gurkört: the leaves and flowers of this herb are used in salads, sausage dishes, and sauces.

Hagdahl, Charles Emil: 1809–1897, doctor, legendary author of Swedish cookbooks and the founder of modern day Swedish cooking.

hasselbackspotatis: oven-fried potatoes where each potato is slit in many fine slices but the bottom of the potato remains intact (gives the potato a slightly fan-like appearance).

havregryn: oatmeal

havskräfta: a type of lobster found in the North Sea off the coast of Norway.

herrgårdsost: a round, porous, Swedish hard cheese, usually aged 10–12 months.

herrgårdsstek: a pot roast of beef served together with cream gravy.

hetvägg: a traditional lenten bun filled with almond paste, whipped cream, and sometimes warm milk.

hovdessert: "marängswiss;" a dessert based on meringues, whipped cream, and chocolate sauce.

hushållsost: a grainy, porous, and mild hard cheese from Sweden.

husmanskost: simple, well-prepared, everday homecooking, often having a long tradition

hökarpanna: a type of casserole that is made from kidney, fillet of pork, onion, and potatoes.

inläggningssill: pickled herring

isgädda: pike caught in the spring during its spawning season.

islandssill: large, oily herring found in the Arctic Ocean north of Iceland. Suitable for pickling.

ister: (sold as absolutely pure cooking fat), melted and strained lard from pigs.

Jansson's frestelse: Swedish national dish made from potatoes, anchovies, onion, cream, and spices. The dish is probably named after the opera singer, Pelle Jansson, 1844–1889.

joppesallad: a salad composed of shrimp, champignons, asparagus, hard-boiled eggs, tomatoes, and shredded lettuce, combined in desired proportions.

kabeljo: lightly dried, boneless, well-salted meat from either cod or ling. Pre-soaked before preparation. Can be boiled, fried, fried in deep-fat, or baked in the oven as a type of casserole.

kaffegrädde: light cream (half and half)

kaggost: a Swedish hard cheese that is grainy, porous, and has a soft consistency.

kallskuret: coldcuts. thin slices of meat, game, poultry, sausage, paté, etc. that are attractively garnished and arranged together with other complementing foods.

kallskål: 1. Former name for bread soaked in a mild beer-like beverage. 2. Fruit or wine punch served cold in a large punch bowl.

kalvdans: cheescake-like dish made from raw milk (the first milk given after calving).

kalvjärpar: small rolls of ground veal filled with parsley.

kams: a speciality from Norrland, a type of dumpling made from barley flour, sometimes also with boiled potatoes.

kapprock: food wrapped in paper or aluminum foil and baked either on the stove or in the oven ("baked in a jacket").

kaviar: fish roe

kejsarhummer: "havskräfta" from the North Sea having a somewhat sweet flavor. Only the tails are used for cooking. Is sold fresh, frozen, or in a can.

kejsarkronor: "the imperial crown," a type of deep-fat fried baked good that uses a special iron.

klappkräm, klappgröt: old-fashioned dessert consisting of sweetened berry juice and semolina.

klenät: fried bake goods, a typical Christmas cookie eaten together with whipped cream and jam or as a complement to compote or Christmas "glögg."

klimp: a dough-like dumpling served with soup. Made from flour, eggs, spices, and flavored with almond, cheese, or parsley.

knäckebröd: crispbread

kolbulle: old-fashioned pancake-like dish, fried over the open fire in lard. Served with fried pork.

kompott: compote.

korngryn: barley

kornmjöl: barley flour.

korvkaka: old-fashioned Swedish home-cooking, a type of cake-like dish made from ground liver, rice or barley pudding, eggs, spices, and often raisins.

krikon: an old plum sort having a sour taste.

kroppkaka: Swedish homecooking, made from mashed or grated potatoes and pork.

kruska: a grainy porridge made from different types of grain, seeds, and dried fruit.

krusmynta: one of many types of mint used for flavoring and garnishing.

krås: giblets, – neck, stomach, heart, and liver from domestic or wild poultry.

kräftsmör: a type of fat that tastes of crayfish, made from parts of the shell and cooking fat.

kummin: spice(seed), cultivated in Sweden but also imported. Has a strong aroma and sharp taste. Used primarily in flavoring bread, cheese, sauerkraut, etc.

kvitten: fruit shaped like a pear, after preparation has a nice, little sourish taste. Good for making jelly and marmelade.

kärnmjölk: milk that remains after churning butter.

lake: salt solution for preserving food.

landgång: single portion, long rectangular open-faced sandwich topped with 3–4 bands of different types meat, fish, cheese and fruit.

lappkok: a complete dinner based on reindeer meat. For example, it can be comprised of grated reindeer liver in reindeer bouillon, finely sliced tongue, followed by boiled reindeer marrow. Complete the dinner with crushed cloudberries and cream.

lertallriksill: a very old dish from Skåne made with salt herring, red onion, green herbs, and browned butter.

lev: an oval loaf of bread made from wheat or other types of grain.

limpa: rye bread that has corn syrup as one if its ingredients.

luad ål: salted, smoked eel, served warm. Sometimes barbequed or broiled.

lufsa: pork pudding or casserole from Öland.

lungmos: a mixture of onions, spices, barley or rice, together with ground liver, lung, or heart that is boiled in bouillon.

lussekatt: Christmas bun baked from saffrons dough.

lutfisk: dried codfish that has been pre-soaked prior to preparation.

långkål: kale in whitesauce that has been boiled in bouillon, a speciality from Halland.

långmjölk, tätmjölk: processed sour milk product having special attributes, comes from Norrland.

läfsa, lefsa: unleavened bread baked over the coals, common in Värmland and Norway.

lättmjölk: low-fat milk (0.5%).

löjrom: whitefish roe

majsmjöl: cornflour

malört: a type of herb that has a very strong aromatic taste. Most often used to flavor schnapps but can also be used to spice sauces, soups, and ground meat.

mannagryn: semolina

matjessill: a lightly salted, spiced, rich herring originating from Holland.

matlagningsmjöl: all-purpose flour

medisterkorv: a lightly smoked boiled sausage of better quality. Suitable for boiling and frying.

medwurst: straight, thick sausage, either boiled or smoked, used mostly as sandwich meat.

mejram: domestic herb having a special aromatic taste and aroma. A common spice found in sausage and other special types of cured meats and delicatessen products. Also used in certain meat dishes featuring light meat as well as yellow pea soup.

mellanmjölk: a low-fat milk (1.5%)

mesost: a cheese made from the whey of cheese .

mjöl: flour

mjölk: milk

mumma: table beverage, especially at Christmas. Made from a mixture of porter, beer, "sockerdricka"(a Swedish soft-drink similar to Seven-up), and spices.

munkar: doughnuts, can be filled with applesauce. Formerly "munkar" were small, thick fried pancakes ("munkpanna"–munk griddle).

måttsats: standerized measuring cups in spoon format used for food preparation. 1 dl = 100 ml, 1 msk = 15 ml, 1 tsk = 5 ml, 1 krm = 1 ml. One should always use level measures.

norrlandspölsa: see "pölsa"

näbbgädda: garfish, edible fish with green bones.

nässelkål: nettle soup

nätting: a type of lamprey, shaped like an eel found in both fresh and salt water.

nävgröt: provincial dish from Värmland. Made from toasted oatmeal and often served with fried pork. The porridge should be so thick it can be "eaten by the handfuls"

ostkaka: provincial dish made from milk with many variations.

palt: special dish from Norrland having many local variations. Can be made from grated, raw potato, barley, rye, or wheat flour, sometimes with fresh blood as one of the ingredients.

paltbröd: round black bread made from blood and flour.

patentsmörgås: slice of fried white bread topped with fried smoked ham, tomato, and a fried egg.

pepparkakor: Swedish gingersnaps

pimpinella: old-fashioned name for aniseed . Used for spicing bread and beverages).

potatiskorv: See Värmlandskorv.

potatismjöl: potato flour

pytt i panna: special Swedish dish made from a mixture of diced boiled potatoes, leftover meat, and onions that are fried in a fry pan on top of the stove. Served together with fried eggs, pickled beets, and HP-sauce.

pärlsocker: nib sugar

pölsa: barley or rice mixed together with onions, spices, and ground liver, lungs, or heart and boiled in bouillon. Norrlands "pölsa" contains a better quality of meat.

raggmunk: potato dish made from grated raw potatoes, milk, flour, and eggs. Served with fried pork.

regnbåge, regnbågslax: farmed salmon

rimma, rimsalta: lightly salted meat or fish for preserving for a short time

risgryn: rice

ris à la Malta: rice pudding mixed with cream, vanilla, and pieces of orange.

rollmops: spicy pickling solution for herring or Baltic herring.

rotmos: old-fashioned dish made from turnips, potatoes, and carrots. Usually served with lightly salted meat or sausage.

rågmjöl: rye flour

rågsikt: rye and wheat flour

råraka: dish made from grated raw potatoes mixed with water or milk and flour.

rökt salt kaviar: smoked, lightly salted fish roe

sagosoppa: soup made from thicken berry juice, often with raisins or dried fruit and thickened with cornstarch.

salta biten: pressed lightly salted beef brisket in a tin.

salt kaviar: salted fish roe

salt sill: salt herring

semla, hetvägg, fettisdagsbulle, fastlagsbulle: traditional lenten bun filled with almond paste and whipped cream. Often served with warm or cold milk.

senap: mustard, a spicy mixture of ground black, yellow, or white pepper, vinegar, sugar etc. Swedish mustard has a mild, sweet flavor.

sillbullar: homecooking with a long tradition, patties made from ground salt herring, meat leftovers, and onion. Served traditionally with raisin sauce.

sirap: light corn syrup

sjurygg: salt water fish from the inner part of the North Sea near Southern Sweden (Stenbit = male, Kvabba = female).

sjuskinnsgröt: an old name used for rice pudding filled with layers of a cinnamon-sugar mixture .

skarpsill, vassbuk, brissling: a small herring which is used for the canning of anchovies and sardines in Sweden.

skarpsås: mayonnaise-like mustard sauce.

skirat smör: melted butter or margarine that is used as a "sauce" for boiled fish or vegetables.

skånsk potatis: raw creamed potatoes seasoned with onion.

slarvsylta: ground brawn made from scraps of brawn leftover from the making of veal, pork, or collared brawn

slottstek: a pot roast of beef with cream gravy seasoned with anchovies.

sluring: an old name for Tuesday soup = vegetable soup with pork broth or lightly salted pork.

småfranska: rolls

småkakor: cookies or biscuits

smålandsdoppa: old-fashioned dish consisting of pork and onion sauce with peeled, boiled potatoes.

smör: butter

socker: sugar

solöga, fågelbo: a little appetizer or luncheon dish comprised of anchovies, pickled beets, onions, and a raw egg yolk.

sotare: Baltic herring fried over coals or lightly broiled.

spettekaka, festkaka: from Skåne. Cake batter made from many eggs and sugar. Baked over an open fire on a revolving iron cone.

spicken: salted, sometimes smoked, food served without cooking (for example, "spickekorv"-sausage, "spickeskinka"-ham).

spiskummin: "ostkummin", seeds used to spice and flavor cheese and baked goods.

standardmjölk: whole milk (3%)

struva: deep-fat fried baked good that requires the use of a decoratively shaped iron.

ströbröd: dried breadcrumbs

strösocker: refined sugar, castor sugar

stångryttare: dried and perhaps smoked grainy sausage

surdeg: old-fashioned sour dough used as a leavening agent when baking. Can be made artificially today.

tisdagssoppa: See sluring.

tistron: black currants

Toast Skagen: lightly fried slice of bread topped with shrimp, whitefish caviar, and a mayonnaise sauce.

torskrom: cod roe

tutti-frutti: a mixture of different fruits, often in simple syrup.

tätmjölk: "långmjölk," a processed sour milk product having special attributes.

tätört: a small herb which was formerly used to sour the milk in "tätmjölk."

Wallenbergare: patties of finely ground veal, sometimes mixed together with egg yolks and cream. Recipe comes from Amelia Wallenberg, daughter to Charles Emil Hagdahl, the founder of modern cuisine in Sweden.

Warg, Christina (Cajsa): (1703–1769), well-known recipe collector, creator of recipes, and author of cookboks.

vattenlingon: old-fashioned method for preserving lingon and green, unripened gooseberries. Put clean lingonberries in glass bottles or jars. Fill with clean, fresh water and cap. If kept in a cool place, the berries will stay fresh for a long time.

vetebullar: coffee rolls.

vetemjöl: all-purpose flour

vispgrädde: whipping cream

våfflor: waffles, baked with a waffle iron and usually served with coffee or as a dessert together with sugar, jam, or whipped cream. Can also be served as an appetizer with salted caviar, anchovies or herring, and sour cream.

värmlandskorv: special sausage that is boiled, made from ground pork and beef, raw potatoes, and spices.

västerbottenost: grainy, porous hard cheese from Sweden of high quality.

västkustsallad: classical Swedish shellfish dish, among other things, consisting of shrimp, mussels, (lobster), champignons, lettuce, and tomatoes.

ägg eggs

ängamat: creamed soup made from the first summer garden vegetables.

änglamat: dessert made from whipped cream mixed with scraps of cake and rusks, together with a little jam.

ärtor, gula: yellow split-peas

Ölandskroppkakor: dumplings made from potato dough that contains grated raw and boiled potatoes.

Ölsupa: old-fashioned gruel-like dish made from "svagdricka," milk, flour, egg yolks, and spices.

Recipe Index

Swedish Index